THE CIRCLE OF PROFIT

ANIK SINGAL

THE CIRCLE OF PROFIT
Copyright © 2016 by Anik Singal

Lurn, Inc. 12410 Milestone Center Drive, Suite 600, Germantown, MD 20876, Second Edition
www.lurn.com
ISBN-10: 1523693673
ISBN-13: 978-1523693672

WHAT YOU'RE ABOUT TO MASTER

The Circle of Profit is the business system that allows anyone in the world to quickly build a profitable business empire right from their laptop.

You can generate millions of dollars simply by giving away information. You're about to learn how to take a topic you love and share it with the world - while creating millions of dollars.

It does not matter if you have never considered being in business for yourself.

It does not matter if you have no experience.

All that matters is that you want more from your life, your career or your financial position. If you want a life of financial freedom, then this is the book for you.

Author Anik Singal is about to take you on his jaw-dropping, 13 year long journey, starting with nothing but a big dream in college and stumbling into the world of online entrepreneurship.

He had no technical knowledge, no experience, and absolutely no idea what he was doing.

But he soon became addicted to the idea of creating wealth using the Internet. That's what this book is all about.

Anik Singal has dedicated his life to learning how someone can spend every moment living their passion - and how they can create a living with it too.

In this second edition of The Circle of Profit you will see that Anik Singal is a true teacher at heart. He not only made sure to share the most up to date information with you but also included over 20 video breaks to show you just how easy this business can be.

If you've ever dreamed of having more in your life, The Circle of Profit is exactly the system to get you there.

ABOUT THE AUTHOR: ANIK SINGAL

Anik Singal started his online business over 13 years ago right from his dorm room. He had absolutely no experience. He stumbled into the world of information marketing by mistake.

After 18 months of struggling through mistakes and missteps, he was just about to give up when he finally broke the first part of the code.

Within just six years - and all from the comfort of his laptop - he built a $10 million a year business which was operating around the world.

His journey was not easy. He experienced many ups and downs. He made millions - and lost millions. He nearly went bankrupt while mastering the formula presented in The Circle of Profit. But it was this journey that has led to the world's #1 rated digital publishing system – the very same system that has gone on to change thousands of lives around the world.

Since he started teaching this system, Anik Singal has been featured in BusinessWeek as a Top Young Entrepreneur. His Internet business has been featured as an Inc. 500 company for two years in a row, all using the same business systems that he teaches now.

Anik Singal has spoken as a motivational and entrepreneurship coach for thousands of people on stages from Singapore to London to Washington DC. He has influenced the lives of thousands by developing and sharing the simple yet powerful system responsible for his great success.

During his career, Anik Singal has sold over $100 million worth of digital information online – all by using the simple model presented to you in The Circle of Profit.

He has now made it his personal mission to create over 1,000 digital publishing entrepreneurs who will take their passion and transform it into an amazing entrepreneurial venture that leads to their financial freedom.

If you're ready to make a big change, join in Anik's journey. Take charge of your financial freedom by using The Circle of Profit.

DEDICATION

I dedicate this book to everyone who has supported and inspired me. My family. My parents, my wife, my sister, brother in law and two wonderful nephews. You provide me the endless support I need to go seize the day. You understand my crazy dreams and you push me forward as I chase them! Thank you.

To my friends. When life gets tough, you are always there to cheer me up. Even when I disappear for months at a time immersed in something, when I come back you are right there smiling and ready to receive me. Thank you for being such amazing friends. I could never do it without you.

To my team. Where do I start? None of my crazy dreams would ever come true if I did not have your support and hard-work. I am constantly amazed at your talent, dedication & integrity. Thank you so much for supporting me no matter how hard it gets! You guys rock!

This book, I dedicate to all of you!

Anik Singal

TABLE OF CONTENTS

FOREWORD

The world's message to everyone is clear, to be successful you must go to school, get good grades, get a safe secure job, save money and invest in your 401(k). That is a great message if you want to become trapped in the rat race.

For decades I have been fighting that message. I've been championing the need for financial education. I've been shouting that the world needs more entrepreneurs and less employee drones. I've been delivering this message in books and from stage since 1997 when I wrote Rich Dad Poor Dad. But I'm getting old. I am so grateful that I met Anik Singal.

Anik is a young man who has picked up my mission and renewed its strength with his infinite energy. Anik is doing the things that I used to do as a young man. He's putting on workshops and seminars. I'm the old guy and Anik is the new guy. I gave speeches from stage, Anik does the same through the internet. Same message, but a new way to deliver and to millions more.

This is why I call Anik one of my most important friends. He is a young man with a vision of the future. Anik is near and dear to my heart, not just because he's picked up the megaphone, but because while so many people go into business just to make money, Anik started his business to solve problems and to make the world a better place.

The world needs entrepreneurs. The world needs people who are responsible for themselves and reliant on themselves. We don't need more employees who are victims to their boss or trapped by their need of a paycheck. We need entrepreneurs who solve problems.

We need entrepreneurs who are honest, moral and ethical. We need entrepreneurs who make the world better. That is why Anik wrote this book. The reason Anik can write this book is because he is the best at digital entrepreneurship. He makes tens of millions of dollars and breaks digital sales records regularly. Anik is the best of the best.

The world is no longer safe for employees. There is no such thing as a safe and secure job. The government is broke and won't be able to support social security or Medicare. The world won't take care of you. You have to do that. And now you can.

With the invention of the personal computer and the Internet the world of business is at your fingertips. All you need now is knowledge. You need that teacher who can show you the path to freedom through entrepreneurship and the Internet. Anik and this book can guide you along the exciting path of entrepreneurship.

I urge you to read this book and to place its knowledge into action. Using this knowledge will free you from the employee trap and prevent you from depending on a government that won't be able to help you. You must save yourself. Anik can help. Read this book.

– Robert Kiyosaki
Bestselling Author of Rich Dad Poor Dad

THE DIGITAL PUBLISHING OPPORTUNITY IS HUGE

DIGITAL PUBLISHING ON THE RISE

EBOOK SALES
IN THE U.S. (IN BILLIONS)

$0.1B
$1B

2015 — $6.74B

2010 — $1.52B

PROFIT MARGINS
(ON AVERAGE)

Digital Publishing — 85%
Physical Product — 10-20%

E-READER USERS
WORLD-WIDE (IN MILLIONS)
60
50
40
30
20
10
2010 '11 '12 '13 '14 '15

"NONTRADITIONALLY-PUBLISHED" EBOOKS
FROM INDIE SELF-PUBLISHERS & AMAZON PUBLISHING IMPRINTS
MAKE UP 58% OF ALL KINDLE EBOOKS PURCHASED IN THE U.S.
(AS OF SEPTEMBER 2015)

58%

100%
80%
60%
40%
20%

Feb '14   May '14   Jul '14   Oct '14   Jan '15   May '15   Sept '15

MARKET SHARE
OF KINDLE STORE EBOOK
$ AUTHOR EARNINGS

Non-Traditional Publishing

Traditional Publishing

PREFACE:
WHAT IS DIGITAL PUBISHING?
THE 40,000 FOOT OVERVIEW

Think about it.

In today's world, what is the #1 asset anyone can have?

It's information.

Google has become one of the biggest companies in the world. Why? Because it provides information.

Now think about why you are ever on the Internet. In other words, what are you really doing when you're online?

Other than email and social media, you're almost always there for information.

Ninety percent of the time that we turn to the Internet is because we are looking for an answer to a question, a solution to a problem, or to learn more about something. It's easy to see why information is the #1 driver of Internet use in the 21st century.

Digital publishing is, quite simply, the three steps you take to monetize information. The Circle of Profit system guides you through the entire system, step by step:

1. Find a topic.
2. Gather information.
3. Monetize information.

First, we start by helping you understand how to choose the right topic for you. There is a very logical, mathematical approach to picking the right topic.

Passion alone is not enough. You have to be sure it's going to be a profitable topic.

Second, we walk you through the various steps of "gathering information." You do not have to be the originator of this information, and you don't have to create it from scratch. You just have to know the right steps to "gathering" information into one place so that it's in an easy-to-digest format.

Third, we dive deep into monetizing that information. There are countless ways to turn information into profit. We focus on the two most important ones - and we call them The Two Phases.

Phase 1 – Earn Commissions By Being The Middle Man (Affiliate Marketing)

This is simple. You get paid large sums of money for recommending other people's information. You never have to create or gather your own information. This is the fastest way to get your business started.

Phase 2 – Create Your Own Online Course (Digital Publishing)

This is where the potential millions are made. We walk you through the steps to gathering information into one location - and then selling access to it. At this point, you will invest a small amount of time to create your own online course.

No matter what phase you are in, you need to learn the basics of how to:
- Logically and mathematically choose the right topic
- Strategically gather information
- Define and locate your market
- Generate traffic
- Monetize by selling your information products to your market, whether they are your products or simply products that you recommend.

Digital publishing is the one business model that cannot go anywhere.

It's here to stay.

No matter what the economy is doing, no matter what the world is doing, the historical performance of digital publishing has shown nothing but growth. The world will always need great information - and will always pay a great price for it.

The key is to get yourself positioned in the right place.

I have the entire system down to a T. It's crucial that you keep an open mind, work hard, and follow my proven formula. Don't try to get creative or re-invent the wheel. (Believe me, it's not worth the trouble and it'll only delay your success.)

The system I have created is very unique. It has been thoroughly time-tested all over the world. For you to really understand its power, you need to understand how I discovered it.

SECTION 1: THE CIRCLE OF PROFIT
YOUR PASSION, YOUR LIFE

CHAPTER 1: MY STORY

In the coming pages, you're going to discover the system that will completely change your life. This system is a simple circle, but it's powerful: Once you master it, your dream life will be at your fingertips.

I know that might sound a bit hard to believe. Trust me: I have lived my life bombarded with crazy claim after crazy claim. I've heard it all in my 13 years as an online entrepreneur.

But what you're reading now is not hype, and it's not exaggeration.

It's a true story with a detailed system that has worked for me and for countless Lurn students as well. All I ask is that you keep an open mind, read every word in this book, take action, and work hard. (And always remember that my entire Lurn Team is here to support you!)

My #1 goal is to teach you the system that will finally give you freedom. You are going to find a topic you love, gather information on it, and turn it all into an amazing virtual business that you can run from anywhere in the world - right on your laptop.

The moment you picked up this book, you empowered yourself with possibly the greatest-kept secret to pure financial freedom.

What you're about to get your hands on is simple and fast. It is a powerful circle that represents a system that can lead to a very profitable and fulfilling (passion) digital business.

A (passion) digital business is a lifestyle business that lets you generate an unlimited amount of income simply by teaching, educating, and immersing yourself in a topic of your choice.

What makes your heart leap? It can be a hobby, a skill, or even a professional trade. I'm going to show you how to build an information business around that topic. The number of possible profitable topics are countless and the subject matter ranges all the way from video gaming, golfing, losing weight, even baking apple pies.

If you have even a hint of knowledge on a topic that interests you, you can build a million-dollar business in almost no time. The key is in having the right system, or in this case, the right circle.

I'm going to show you how to use the power of the Internet - in an automated fashion that requires zero technical expertise - to:

- Find others who share your passion on any topic.
- Create a great relationship with them.
- Begin to generate thousands (or even millions) of dollars by simply helping them excel.

The truth is that the sky is the limit. You can scale deep into a specific topic and keep growing, or you can launch multiple digital publishing businesses by going into many different topics.

I've chosen to use the Circle of Profit to build multiple companies now. All of my companies are 100% virtual. I travel 70% of the year and generate close to $20 million in sales every year. I have countless students who have copied my lifestyle and business – and they're all doing amazingly well.

The beauty of the Circle is that it lets you build your business around your life. That's why I call it a "lifestyle business."

How big your circle grows is completely up to you.

JIMMY'S STORY

Throughout my business life and travels, I meet all kinds of people who share their stories with me. The following story is about a friend of mine, Jimmy Kim. This is an amazing story that shows the raw power of being a digital publisher.

I met Jimmy in Las Vegas. We didn't meet for work. Not even close. He was actually a friend of a friend. We all happened to be in Vegas at the same time. Over the days that we got to know each other, he became very curious about what I did for a living. (These were the days after I had really mastered the digital publishing system.)

The more I got to know him, the more I understood that Jimmy worked way harder than I ever did. I admired that about him a lot - until I met him one day after work.

Jimmy had spent 16 hours working that day. He came home looking half-dead.

Jimmy was ridiculously successful. Still in his 20s, he was the youngest General Manager of a car dealership. And what I found most amazing was that he had climbed the ranks from washing cars all the way up to running the entire dealership!

Impressive, right?

The problem was that all that success came at a steep price. I watched Jimmy sacrifice his personal life on a daily basis. He worked weekends and holidays. He took only one vacation a year.

At the same time, Jimmy would watch me live my life. I traveled the world. I loved my life. I lived the dream, as he used to say.

One day, he had finally had enough.

He came to me and insisted that I show him what I was doing. He wanted to know if he could follow the same steps, the same system and become a successful digital publisher.

By then he had become one of my closest friends, so I took a weekend and laid it all out for him. What I shared with him was exactly what I am sharing with you in this book. Actually, I only taught him part of what I'm teaching you, so you're going to know even more.

Within just weeks, Jimmy had launched his online business and was already generating a profit!

A few months later, Jimmy was making $3,000 to $4,000 a month, while still working a few part time hours. After that, he never looked back. He worked my system harder and harder.

His business exploded and today he runs a multi-million dollar empire. He lives in his dream home in California. He drives expensive cars and takes about ten vacations a year.

You see, what Jimmy did was simple.

Phase 1 – He built an email list of subscribers.

Immediately after I shared the system with him, he dove into Phase 1 by building an email list of subscribers. He would send them a simple email every day, and in those emails, he would endorse a product.

For every sale he got, he made a commission!

Over time, his email list got bigger and bigger. The bigger the list got, the more he earned. He kept growing his email list until it was over 10,000 subscribers and he was earning over $10,000 a month.

That was when it was time for Phase 2 for him.

Phase 2 – He built his own digital product.

Jimmy's very first product launch generated over $52,000 in just 7 days. His business grew from that one product launch to many. Today, his average product launch generates over $1 million.

He is now the CEO of SendLane, one of the world's leading email autoresponder companies. He is also invested in many other companies, in which he uses online marketing to transform the company.

Just imagine. All this began with him building a small email list so that he could make an additional income.

This is exactly the path that I want to put you on.

A DREAM ALMOST FORGOTTEN

I grew up in a traditional Indian family where education and professional careers were always the ultimate goal. I was surrounded by incredibly successful engineers, doctors, and lawyers.

My own father is a very successful engineer to whom I owe every bit of my success. He always pushed me to excel, teaching me that there is no replacement for hard work.

In the Indian community, the utmost respect is given to doctors. Parents dream of their children becoming doctors. Growing up in this environment, I naturally wanted to become a doctor.

But I never had a strong basis for this dream.

I had observed that doctors got a tremendous amount of respect. I also knew that doctors were wealthy and lived comfortable lives - and that was important to me ever since I was a child.

I proudly declared to everyone that I wanted to become a doctor.

But deep down, I knew I had a big problem: School had never come easy for me.

Now, I always did well in school because I consistently supplemented the required work with a boatload of even more hard work. I lived by a mantra of making myself and those around me proud. If I had to stay up all night studying, I did.

My parents had instilled in me some very strong principles: Work hard, never quit, and fight for your dreams. Using these simple teachings, I worked my way through school.

Having immigrated to the U.S. in the third grade (and barely able to speak English) I burned the midnight oil all the way to the top of my high school class.

After reaching the top of my high school class, I put all of my dedication for the next two years into one of the best pre-medical programs in the world. As far as I knew, my dream was nearly realized.

I felt like I was well on my way. The heavy lifting was almost over. I was in such a highly regarded pre-med program that I was virtually guaranteed admission to any top medical school when I was ready.

Everyone around me was glowing with pride. I would get endless praise day in and day out for my achievement. I should have been content, excited, and fulfilled.

But even with all my dreams so close, I was plagued by a pestering, nagging empty space in my heart. Every night, I fell asleep staring at the ceiling. Every morning, I struggled to climb out of bed. I was tortured by the thought of going to class the next day.

I was bored out of my mind. I had absolutely zero passion for what I was studying.

As the months passed, the feelings grew stronger. The unhappy voice inside me got so loud one day that I could not ignore it anymore. I knew it was not just a passing phase.

I had a serious problem on my hands.

Determined not to become a person who is perpetually miserable with their life choices, I took an entire day to sit down, close the door, and force myself to consider my discontent. I promised myself that I would not leave the room until I discovered the true reason behind my troubled heart.

And that night, I did find the reason.

I kept reflecting back into my past. I took a mental journey to my childhood. There I discovered the passion that had been in my heart the whole time even though I had somehow been able to completely ignore it: Creation!

Creation! Ever since I was a child, I had been mesmerized by creation. I was never the kind to simply follow orders or to do things the way everyone else did them.

I was the neighborhood kid who set up the lemonade stand - but I didn't just set up a stand; I hired younger kids to run the stand while I sat inside watching cartoons. I was the kid who scoffed at being told what I couldn't do and rejoiced in my ability to prove the scoffer wrong.

Lost in the dream of impressing everyone around me, I had ignored my true feelings. I had forgotten that all I'd ever wanted was to create and control my own destiny. I wanted to build my own future. I wanted to be the one in control.

As far back as I could remember, I used to make a very bold statement to all my friends. I used to say, "I'll be making over $10,000 a month by the time I graduate from college." I didn't just say this once or twice; I repeated it often. I genuinely believed it.

As you can imagine, people laughed at me all the time. I was ridiculed. I was constantly questioned. But none of that mattered to me. I never knew how I was going to do it; I just knew that I would.

Well, that night I realized that becoming a doctor did not fit my dream. Don't get me wrong; I have immense respect for doctors. They have saved my life countless times. It just wasn't going to be the right profession for me.

My disturbing realization

I came to another realization that night too - but this one was disturbing. I was going to have to change my path. I was going to have to leave this amazing pre-med program that made my parents beam with pride. I was going to venture out into the world of business where I had no guidance, no mentorship, and absolutely no resources.

The thought of sharing this news with my parents was the most frightening experience of my life. I kept imagining the disappointment that would come over them. In their eyes, and the eyes of everyone else around me, I was living the dream.

I was sure that my parents would be devastated with my decision, and that everyone else would laugh and call me crazy.

So there I was at the most critical juncture of my life.

THE MOMENT OF TRUTH

I went to my parents in great fear. I had decided to tell them that I wanted to drop this so-called "perfect life" and go into a life full of (in their eyes) "sharks and monsters".

To my stunned surprise (yet enormous relief), I discovered just how amazing my parents were when I told them. Incredibly, they blessed my decision and reinforced their support of me, saying that my life and dreams were mine and mine alone.

I had just easily won the first major battle toward the life of my dreams, but I knew that this was just the beginning. The hard part was still ahead.

What was I going to do now?

I had two years to make good on my public declaration. I had two years to dive into a world I knew nothing about. I had two years to fulfill my mission of making $10,000 a month by the time I graduated from college.

The clock was ticking.

$100 IN MY BANK ACCOUNT

I sat and pondered what I was going to do. I had exactly $100 to my name. My options - and my funds - were very limited. It wasn't like I could just go out and buy a McDonald's franchise.

Speaking of franchises, I then spent many hours researching them. I wanted to launch a franchise because they give you an entire system, step by step. I had always heard that "anyone" can run a franchise as long as they work hard and follow the steps.

Well, my research quickly revealed something to me: Any franchise that was worth the effort or that I really liked required a minimum $100,000 investment.

I spent hours looking and the lowest-priced franchise I could find was $25,000 - and anything at that investment level did not sound like it would perform well.

I had $100 in my bank account. I was a long way from $100,000. I was deflated.

"What now?"

That was it. Opening a franchise was all I could come up with. It felt like my journey had ended before it even began! If I could not buy a franchise, then what in the world was I going to do?

And that was the first time I felt the real electricity of being an entrepreneur.

It was one thing to want to be an entrepreneur.

It was a completely different thing to find an opportunity. Wanting to start my own business and take control of my own life was not going to be enough.

I had to actually find what I was going to do. I had to take action.

To make matters worse, I had nowhere to turn for advice. I didn't know anyone who was in business for themselves. I was all alone and feeling completely lost.

And then I thought of one "friend" who might be able to offer me a ray of hope.

That friend's name?

Google.com

MY LIFE CHANGING GOOGLE SEARCH

I ran straight to Google and typed in these cliché words:

Google	how to make money	🔍

What happened after that was very frustrating. I was electronically ushered into scam after scam. I read about exciting, moneymaking envelope-stuffing opportunities! I learned about multiple life-changing MLM network marketing companies - but they all seemed to magically disappear in weeks. I was even taken in (for a few minutes) by a scam claiming that I could make good money simply by filling out surveys.

But I only had $100 to invest, so I took some time to research these "opportunities" and quickly found that they were not real.

Something inside me told me to keep searching. Something told me that the answer was just around the corner, and if I quit now, all my efforts would be wasted.

As I kept my search on, I finally landed on a forum that was dedicated to "online entrepreneurs."

Hmm. Online entrepreneur.

Now, what in the world is that? What's an "online entrepreneur"?

I started reading forum post after forum post and became absolutely enthralled with what I was seeing. Day after day, I was communicating with people on this forum who were claiming (and proving) that they were making anywhere from $300 a day and up to even $10,000 a day! They were all doing this sitting at home, using just one computer. They had no employees, no offices, and no headaches.

They seemed honest, genuine, and very helpful. I was sold. These entrepreneurs were cashing in big time by just publishing information on the Internet and selling it using some simple models. There wasn't just one person doing it; there were hundreds!

That was the day I decided on my new career. I was going to be an online entrepreneur.

EIGHTEEN MONTHS WASTED AND $100 LOST

Unfortunately, back when I started in 2002, there was no system like The Circle of Profit with step by step instructions that I could follow. Back then, everyone found their own system, by hook or by crook.

Some were fortunate enough to succeed... but most failed.

From what I could see, the formula was very simple.

1. Find a topic you're good at or passionate about.
2. Create an information product about that topic.
3. Put it up online and wait for your millions.

I never stopped to consider the missing pieces. I never stopped to consider that almost all successful businesses were built from models and systems that could be copied. I even forgot that when I first started, I had specifically wanted to start a franchise for this very reason: A step by step system that could be copied.

Big mistake.

In order to make up for the lack of a system, I spent months on the forum educating myself. I asked as many questions as I could and finally, I assumed I had figured the system out.

I never even confirmed if I was right. Instead, I hastily chose a topic I was good at and went ahead blindly.

I spent seven months painfully learning how to execute each step myself. I spent seven months applying techniques as well as I could.

And I spent my $100. I was absolutely sure that I was about to break into the millions.

I was convinced that I had figured out the "niche" that no one else had ever tried. I had no system, no training and no coach, but I rolled up my sleeves and dove right in.

After seven months of hard work, slaving over my computer day in and day out, the moment of truth finally came. This was the day that I would launch my information product and start laughing my way to the bank.

But the day I launched my online business, something crucial was missing.

I wasn't getting a single sale.

24 hours passed with zero sales. A week passed. A month passed. And I had made nothing.

Not only had I spent my $100 but I had even charged $500 on a credit card. For the first time in my life, I was in debt!

I was heartbroken. My dream of instant millions came crashing down. But, as I've already mentioned, I wasn't one to give up that easily. I was determined to find my mistake and try a different model. One way or the other, I was going to succeed as an online entrepreneur.

I had all the determination in the world, but determination didn't give me the crucial thing I needed: A system.

No matter how many months passed and no matter how hard I worked, I continued to fail because I never had a model to follow. I had no one holding my hand.

Seven months became 18 months and I had yet to make a dime in profit. I had worked more than 3,000 hours and had nothing to show for it but debt.

THE FINAL NIGHT – 24 HOURS LEFT…

I was ready to quit. I was embarrassed. Disheartened. Exhausted. I was beginning to think that building a digital publishing business around information products was a dream that was too good to be true.

Had I been scammed yet again? Was business not for me? Should I have stayed the course and become a doctor? What would I tell my parents?

And what about all my friends who couldn't wait to say "I told you so"?

I felt there was nothing left for me to try. That night, I posted on the forum about how disheartened I was and that I was getting ready to call it quits.

A few moments later, a forum member sent me the private message that changed my life. I'll never forget it:

"Kid, I am tired of watching you struggle so much and I do not want to see you quit. I am going to give you a few steps. Spend the next 24 hours doing what I say and I promise it will work. If not, then you can quit."

This was the first time anyone had offered me a "system." I was incredibly suspicious, but I had nothing else to lose.

I thought, "If this doesn't work, then I'm done. I'll go get some J.O.B. and do it the way that everyone else tells me to do it. I'll accept my defeat and never try anything like this again."

That night I worked until 5:00 a.m. I followed his steps exactly.

I remember typing away at my keyboard with my head bobbing up and down, I was barely staying awake. I worked until my last breath and finally retreated to sleep.

This was the final hour. I remember praying. I knew that the next morning would be the key deciding moment in my life.

Six hours later, my eyes opened. I sprang out of bed and nearly fell flat as I plunged towards my computer, still half asleep. I had to know right away. Had it worked?

With chills running down my back, I remember logging into my account to see that I had made $300 in profit while I slept.

I rubbed my eyes and drew my face closer to the screen just to confirm that I was not hallucinating. I wasn't.

For the first time in my life, I had made a profit: My first $300 as an online entrepreneur!

The magical feeling you get when you make that first dollar online is unlike any other. It's hard to explain. It's the very moment you know deep down that your life will never be the same again.

At Lurn, we are very fortunate to have the chance to help thousands of our students achieve that magical breakthrough. As a matter of fact, our current Director of Operations actually started out as one of our students.

She made her first $1 online using Phase 1 of the Circle of Profit.

OLGA'S STORY: MAKING THAT FIRST $1

Olga came to Lurn as a student who had been struggling to succeed online. She knew she wanted to be an online marketer, but she lacked the necessary system. She was interested in digital publishing, but she had one major concern. Olga was an exchange student who had come to the United States from Germany, and English was her third language.

One of Olga's best traits is that she is a fighter. Even though English was her third language, she was very determined to make it. She just needed to find the right system.

When she first got started, she never had anyone show her the ropes. She just learned little pieces here and there and tried to put them together - a lot like I did when I first started.

Needless to say, she struggled. For months.

When she was introduced to the Circle of Profit, she had finally found the very system that helped her make that first $1 online.

She still talks about the chills she felt down her spine when she generated her first $1 in profit. She could not believe her eyes. To this day she says she will never forget that feeling.

That was the day that she knew her wildest dreams were officially possible. She knew without a doubt that the Circle of Profit system was going to help her turn her true passion into $1 million - or even much more.

Today, her business grows every single month. She works on it part-time and sees her income rising day by day. She says she couldn't see herself doing anything different. Ever.

Olga has been so successful, and we were so impressed with her that we invited her to become part of our team. The student has now become the teacher!

THE BIRTH OF THE CIRCLE OF PROFIT

Back to the night I earned my first $300 in commissions... This was a major juncture in my life.

That $300 was more significant than even I knew, because it marked the birth of the Circle of Profit system. Step 1 of Phase 1 had just been discovered.

For 18 months I had tried to make money online. I had used countless strategies and worked well over 3,000 hours trying to generate a profit online. But none of it worked.

Not until I had the right system was I able to make $300 in six hours, all while I was sleeping!

It was shocking and even slightly infuriating to learn that out of everything I had tried, the simplest and easiest model of them all was the one that finally led me to profit.

The time had come to pour my heart and soul into this new strategy, and I wanted to see how far I could push it. I wanted to see just how much I could actually make if I started "rinsing and repeating" the system.

Would I finally make good on my promise to my friends? Could I really make my first $10,000 before I even graduated from college?

FROM THOUSANDS TO MILLIONS

I could easily see the potential in what I had found. My first and foremost goal remained $10,000 a month, but I was already dreaming of the millions I knew could be earned!

I was prepared to work hard. Being conservative, I estimated that it would take me about six months to earn my first $10,000 online.

But much to my surprise, I reached that lifelong dream in only 60 days.

During those first 60 days, I was focused on one thing: I wanted to build as big an email list as possible. In other words, I wanted to have as many newsletter subscribers as possible.

The best part was that I did not need any technical skills to do that. I only needed to put up a one page website!

I began to use simple and automated techniques to attract visitors to my site. My one page website would then convert them into subscribers for me. It made so much sense. I was basically attracting hundreds of people who had the same passion as me. When they reached my website, I simply offered them a free PDF report or audio recording in exchange for their email address.

With a simple promise and some automated work to get visitors landing on my website, I began to collect thousands of email addresses. My subscriber list began to grow daily all on its own!

The model I followed was as simple as it gets:

My next step was to build a relationship with my new subscribers. I followed a simple pattern of daily emails and before I knew it, I was considered a true expert in my niche!

It's important to note that I was never a good writer. As a matter of fact, writing was the only subject I nearly failed in school. My English teacher once actually told me that my writing work was so horrible that I "would never write for a living."

Ha! Little did she know!

The formula for emailing your subscribers is so simple that your writing ability is really not important. I will show you just what I mean later in this book. For now, just know that it is not enough to get a subscriber; you have to build a relationship with that subscriber. The stronger your relationship, the more income you will earn, and the more secure your business will be.

Here's how quickly my business soared: Within just three months after the night I made my first $300, I was already earning more than $25,000 a month!

At this point, I was still using the same system but I added a slight twist: My own information product. That's it.

Doing this - adding my own information product - literally doubled my income overnight.
Adding my own product did not add any effort or hours to my workload Honestly. If anything, it made my business even easier.

But the increased scale and profit margin it added to my business was absolutely astonishing.

Remember, I was working on a very tight timeline back then. I was still a full-time college student, so I rarely had more than one or two hours a day to invest in my business.

Many Lurn students typically start while they still have full-time jobs. This is a good thing, and one of the most powerful aspects of this system. I actually want you to start out on a part-time basis.

As you grow, you can decide to invest more time in the business depending on how large you'd like to scale it. For me, it was clear. I wanted to create a multi-million dollar business. So the only question left for me was:

"How do I go from $25,000 to $1 million - and then to $10 million?"

Now let's fast-forward a few years.

MY BORING AND REPETITIVE FORMULA TO $10 MILLION

I continued to "rinse and repeat" the same circle formula, and my profits continued to grow. I quickly learned that the key was to simply release more information products. My income would take a major jump every time I expanded my arsenal of online courses.

I could expand in two ways:
1. Offer more information products in the same niche.
2. Offer new digital publishing businesses in different niches.

I did both, but I focused my energy more on expanding my product lineup in one niche. The growth and scale was pretty amazing. It felt like every new information product I added didn't just grow my revenue but it also added scale and sped up the pace at which my business was growing!

Amazingly, within my first year of business, working part time with only three information products and a full-time college schedule, I was able to generate over $1 million in sales.

I was convinced. I could easily grow my business to $10 million. I just had to continue implementing the Circle.

I was living my dream. I had complete financial freedom. My business was literally taking me around the world. I even began getting invitations to speak on stage and tell my story. From Singapore to New York, I was speaking on a new stage almost every other week.

My success continued when I was featured in both BusinessWeek magazine as a Top Young Entrepreneur and by Inc 500 as one of the fastest-growing companies in the United States.

The next six years flew by. Every day I woke up and I put the same system in action. Day after day. The truth is that I was even beginning to get bored. But bored or not, my business was booming.

In less than six years of starting with just $100 in my bank account, I had now created a business that was generating over $10 million a year.

Growing up, $10 million had been my dream. It was my biggest goal. So when I achieved it, I found myself lost. What now?

I decided that if I wanted to hit $100 million, I would have to change things. To this day, I have no idea why I felt that way. I have no idea why I would have abandoned a system that was working near flawlessly. I guess I just felt the system was too simple to be able to generate 9 or even 10 figures. What would happen if I abandoned the Circle of Profit system?

I started to look for a different system. I started abandoning the Circle and making bad decisions. My search was completely unfounded. It was based purely on incorrect assumptions.

And it would prove to be a mistake that nearly cost me my life.

The price of not following The Circle of Profit:

BANKRUPTCY

It had taken me six years to build my business from $100 to $10 million a year. However, generating income had become so simple and repetitive that I actually started seeking other business models. I want to expand my goals and I was convinced that nothing so simple could ever scale the way I wanted.

So what did I do? I began to hire an expensive team. I built offices around the world.

I poured money into becoming what I call a "magazine cover CEO." I wanted to live the jet-set lifestyle of a Fortune 500 CEO. Having had so much success so fast, I began to believe that I was invincible.

Surely, I thought, it wasn't the Circle system that was creating the success but rather my business genius.

I made many changes, most of which turned out to be poisonous to my health and to my business.

In 2008 when the economy crashed, so did I. I had turned a blind eye to the only system that had ever made me millions.

I went from making $10 million a year in sales to nearly bankrupt - and $1.7 million in debt. I owed everyone money: Banks, credit cards, vendors, my family... even my friends.

I found my phone ringing day and night by people to whom I owed money. My debt kept increasing as my expenses shot up. Even though my new path was not paying off and I could clearly see my troubles, I foolishly refused to change the model.

I was in denial. I convinced myself that I just needed to weather the storm. Needless to say, I reached a breaking point. My life slowly began to fall apart. Things got so bad that my physical health was suffering badly. Every other month, I found myself being rushed to the hospital. And as if that wasn't enough, my relationships were collapsing, too.

I was in a complete downward spiral and felt trapped. I did not know how I was going to get out of any of it until...

I NEARLY DIED ON AN AIRPLANE

On one of my flights to India to visit one of my offices, my health took a major dive. I was on a layover in Amsterdam and I began to feel very ill. I could tell something bad was happening. I knew I needed to cancel my trip and get back home as soon as possible.

I remember standing in front of the boarding gate for my next flight and I felt almost as if my body was frozen. I couldn't move. A voice inside me would not let me board my plane.

I stood there at the gate, unmoving, and watched my entire flight board. I watched my plane pull out toward the runway.

I could tell that I had begun to bleed internally, but the thought of visiting a hospital in a foreign country petrified me. I had to find a way to keep myself healthy that night for about 12 hours until the morning when I could fly back to the U.S.

That entire night, I found myself sweating in bed and rapidly deteriorating. (I later discovered that I had actually lost about 50% of my blood volume that night.)

The next morning, I stumbled back to the airport. I made it onto the plane. I was able to board the flight and find my way to my seat. I could feel myself getting sicker and sicker. I gave myself tiny goals and motivated myself to make sure I could hang in there until I reached home.

I don't remember much after that. I do remember the plane pushing back from the gate. I remember sweating profusely. I even vaguely remember the passenger to my left giving me very strange looks. That was my last memory. I must have passed out.

15 minutes later... I was being strapped to a stretcher. I was being carried down stairs and out of the plane. Apparently, the plane had pulled back from the gate just as I lost consciousness.

Fortunately, the passenger next to me had the intuition to see that I was not simply sleeping, but that I had lost consciousness. He apparently waved down the flight attendant and the plane was immediately stopped.

My memory is very spotty after that. I must have lost consciousness again because the next thing I remember is being in a hospital bed connected to multiple devices. There were so many devices on me that I could not even move. That's when I realized that I was alone in a foreign country on what I feared would be my deathbed.

That moment, I remember thinking to myself:

"I became an entrepreneur because of the FREEDOM it provides. What the heck am I doing? This is not freedom at all! I can't even MOVE. I'm literally tied down to this bed and barely alive. This is not what I signed up for.

I need to make changes. NOW."

My family rushed to meet me in Amsterdam. The doctors scrambled to save my life and fortunately, thanks to the amazing medical care, I was able to recover in a few days. After I regained some strength, they cleared me to return home.

That was it. I promised myself that the minute I landed, it was time for me to make a drastic change.

Within days, I began to close every unnecessary business office that I had opened. My business had grown to employ a team of 86 employees. As much as it pained me to let go of almost everyone, I had to.

And the moment had come for me to put my ego aside and figure out just what had gone wrong. Why was I suddenly bankrupt and dying, when only two years ago I had been swimming in millions and living the life of my dreams?

The answer came to me pretty quickly: I had turned my back on The Circle of Profit.

As I sat in my dark office the night before I returned the keys, I made a commitment to myself: I would go back to the Circle of Profit, the simple system that had helped me build my first $10 million. This time, I would not turn my back on it. I refused to declare bankruptcy. Instead, I became motivated to get back to the top and this time, stay there.

BACK TO $10 MILLION IN 16 MONTHS

What happened after that was surreal. I dug my heels in, simplified my business (and my life) and went back to the simple basics of the Circle of Profit. I started all over again.

I went back to Phase 1 and gave it everything I had.

I was $1.7 million in debt. But in only 12 months, I was able to completely pay off that debt. Even better, I found myself again sitting on a $10 million a year business only 16 months after I had decided to go back to the Circle of Profit.

What had once taken me six years to do, I had now done in 16 months.

I decided it was time for me to teach this to the world.

THE MORAL OF THIS STORY

The Circle of Profit is simple and redundant. Use it.

Don't try to reinvent something that works well. Just copy and paste the steps you are taught and focus on your execution.
The simplicity of this Circle is a gift. It is this very gift that allows you to focus on your life while letting the business run itself. You can use the following system to make $100,000 a year, $10 million a year, or even $100 million a year. I have no doubt anymore about the scalability of this system.

From this moment on, your success and your future is completely up to you and only you. If you commit to working hard and being coachable, I commit to guiding you through your journey.

WILLIE'S STORY: HOW I FINALLY QUIT MY BORING JOB

I thought I had finally made it.

For years I had dreamt of having a successful online business. I had enrolled in countless courses and tried everything I could. I barred no expense and invested every penny I could.

But no matter how hard I worked, I could not seem to get the breakthrough I needed.

Even after investing well over $5,000, I had barely earned $200.

After all that hard work, countless hours of my life, and over $5,000 invested, I was nowhere. Nowhere!

I started to have doubts. I was becoming more and more convinced that maybe being an online entrepreneur wasn't for me.

That was when I stumbled across Anik Singal. Anik seemed to be leading a long line of success stories. He himself was generating over

38

$10 million a year using a system that seemed very simple. I didn't know what, but something felt different about him. I was excited.

He was the exact opposite.

Unlike any of the other courses I had experienced, I could immediately tell that Anik really cared. He really wanted to help people like me. I decided to take my life into my own hands and I took action. I became a Lurn student and immediately dove into the Circle of Profit.

It was super simple.

It was almost like copying and pasting what he did. I finally found myself understanding every detail about my business. The best part was that in less than 10 days of following his system, I generated over $1,200!

I had spent months and months to make only $200 and here I was able to use his system to generate over $1,200 in just 10 days! I was hooked.

I worked harder than ever. I learned more. I completed all his training. I always took action. Before I knew it, I quit my job - a job where I had been earning over $80,000 a year!

I've never looked back. I live a completely different life now.
I thank God every day for having found this system and for having become a part of Lurn Nation. Whenever I can, I tell every one I care about that this is the system that will change your life. Take action on it!

Willie Laney
Lurn Student and Coach

Update to Willie Laney's Story
by Anik Singal

Willie has had such great progress that he is now a coach at Lurn Nation. Recently, he moved on to Phase 2 and published his first-ever online course. He was able to generate over $10,000 in his first 30 days.

Now Willie is working on expanding into another niche and releasing his second digital product. Before we know it, he will be one of our greatest success stories.

For those of you at Lurn Nation, you can have Willie coach you. He is in there all the time!

CHAPTER 2: THE DIGITAL GOLD RUSH

In this chapter, I'm going to formally introduce you to the world of digital publishing. You are now going to see the power of building a business based around information.

Just know this: Moving forward, your business is 100% built around information. As a matter of fact, the three main steps you use will be the following:

1. Find other people like you (find a topic).
2. Organize information (put together great information that your market will love).
3. Monetize (pick a business system that allows you to create a profit).

My team and I have worked for years to put this entire system down into simple steps that anyone can copy. Even if you have no experience, no technical background, and you have never considered owning your own business, you can do this.

You will amaze yourself.

But first, you need to understand just how enormous this opportunity is.

THE MODERN DAY GOLD RUSH

There has never been a better time to create this kind of digital publishing business. More and more, people are turning to the Internet for information.

The best part is that these people are not just looking for free information; there are millions around the world happy to pay for it.

I genuinely believe that this is the modern-day California Gold Rush. I'm serious.

Many people make the mistake of thinking that Internet opportunities have come and gone, but they are very wrong. The opportunity to create millions on the Internet with nothing but your computer is alive, well, and ready for the taking. It is actually better than ever before.

Today is an even better day to launch your own online business than it was 10 years ago.

Remember when I started? It took me 18 months just to crack the code. Today, you have the system handed right to you. We have seen our Lurn students create success in as little as 30 days.

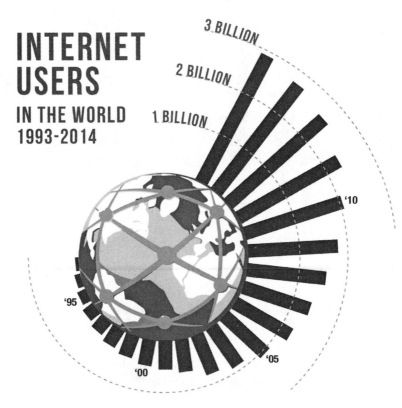

INTERNET USERS
IN THE WORLD
1993-2014

(Source: ResidualIncomer.com)

Consider this: Twenty years ago if you wanted to learn something, you'd go to the library or bookstore and pick up a book. If there was new information on a topic, it had to go through a long publication process - an average of 18 months! By the time that new information came out, it was often already outdated.

Today is very different.

We live in the Information Age. Basically, the greatest industry in the world today is the information industry. Those with access to information and the ability to distribute it the fastest are the ones who are poised to be our next millionaires and billionaires.

The day of physical books is quickly disappearing. And the speed of this transition of information acquisition from physical books to online? That's growing faster than ever, too.

In 2012, Amazon CEO Jeff Bezos announced that Amazon's sales of digital books had surpassed their sales of physical books. Just look at how fast the Internet is growing around the world.

In the last 10 years, the number of people using the Internet has grown by 600%. It's estimated that there are more than three billion people now with access to the Internet.

REVENUE FROM E-BOOK SALES
IN THE U.S. FROM 2008-2018 (IN BILLION U.S. DOLLARS)

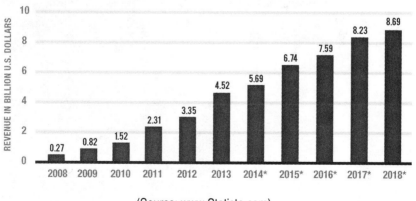

(Source: www.Statista.com)

Even better, studies have shown that over 62% of everyone on the Internet primarily uses it to gain information.

And these numbers continue to grow. It's estimated that by 2020, there will be five billion people online. In the United States, the market for eBooks alone was worth $270 million in 2008. By 2014, that figure had exploded to $5.69 billion.

Do the math. That averages to over 250% growth per year!

At this rate, that number could grow to a staggering $8.69 billion by 2018.

USES OF THE INTERNET
IN PERCENTAGE OF USERS

62.2% Info About Health

62% Research

58% Shopping

50.1% Banking

45.5% Looking For Jobs

43% Travel Reservations

15.2% Meeting People

Imagine having just a tiny sliver of those billions. This is why I'm telling you it's a perfect time to start your digital publishing business.

Just think: This book is a perfect example of the importance and power of information. You have chosen to read this book because you know that the system in it can quickly change your life. Although you and I might never meet face to face, the Internet is allowing me to teach you everything I know (if you bought a digital version or decide to become a Lurn Nation student).

Many of my students are now earning millions - without ever having met me.

WHAT DO YOU NEED TO START?

It's very simple. The only physical tools you need are:

- Access to a computer.
- An Internet connection.
- A minimum one hour a day.

I think it is fair to assume that you already have all three of these tools. If you are reading this book, it's unlikely that you got your hands on it without having both a computer and Internet access. And I firmly believe that we all have at least one hour a day to make our dreams come true.

Here are a few common questions I often get asked about what is needed:

1. Do I need to be an expert or have a degree in my topic or niche?

No. I don't, and it has never made even a tiny impact on my success. In fact, after working with over 100,000 students, I have found that having too much professional education in a topic can make it harder to connect to that very market as a digital publisher.

2. Do I need to know how to build websites or have technical knowledge?

Absolutely not. Today, more than 13 years after I started my business, I still cannot put up my own webpage. The truth is that you can either acquire technical help very inexpensively nowadays using freelancers, or you can use any of the countless automated tools that do that kind of heavy lifting for you.

3. Do I need to quit my job to work on this?

No, you do not. As a matter of fact, I highly recommend that you start this process on a part time basis first and then grow to full time as your income increases. I want you to take a financially safe route to your business.

4. Is it going to cost me a lot of money?

Again, the answer is still no. Obviously, if you have investment capital, it can help speed up the process. However, you can start with very minimal investment - even just a few hundred dollars. You will just need to invest some time and be more patient for your results.

Beyond that, you need resilience and drive. Learn as much as you can and always focus on taking action.

HOW I RAN MY BUSINESS FROM THE I.C.U.

Back in 2005, my business was just starting to scale. I had passed $1 million and was on my way to reach $3 million during my second year in business. However, I had a major event happen in my personal life. Unexpectedly, my physical body started breaking down on me.

I had battled a condition called Crohn's Disease since I was a child. Although it had been well managed for years, it suddenly took a severe turn for the worse. It got so bad that one day, out of the blue, I was admitted to the hospital.

From there things got worse - and fast. I had gone into the hospital expecting to get treated and discharged in three days. Two weeks later I had to be rushed in an ambulance to a specialty hospital. And two days after that I found myself fighting for my life, under 24/7 watch in the Intensive Care Unit.

There I was. One moment I was happily growing and scaling my business. The next moment, I was fighting simply to stay alive. I had bills to pay and expenses that were coming in daily. I did not feel that I had the luxury to just sit idle in the hospital. It just was not my personality.

So, now I was faced with a whole new challenge: How do you run a business from a hospital bed? I was in no condition to get up and use a computer. Even if I could, it wasn't allowed.

Lucky for me I did not have a typical day job. If I had, there is no way my business would have survived. My career would have ended right there, as it was just starting to take off. My income would have fallen to zero almost over night.

But thanks to my simple system, I had (and still have) the luxury of being able to run my business from anywhere in the world. I can run it from home, a coffee shop, the beach and when necessary, even the I.C.U.

Now this next part is a bit funny. I'm smiling just thinking about it.

There were no computers or laptops allowed in the I.C.U. So, here is what I had to do. I had my friend sneak my BlackBerry (iPhones and Androids didn't exist yet) into the I.C.U. and leave it underneath the pillow. Even though it was a tiny device with incredibility limited features, this phone would prove to be the only tool I needed to keep running my entire business.

How did I do it?

Late at night, once the lights were off, I would hide under the covers and secretly use my phone to text and email. In just about an hour a day, I was running and managing my entire business "undercover" literally.

I was in the I.C.U. for over three months, but I was able to run my entire business using just my cell phone. I generated over $450,000 in sales, all while I could barely stand up without my heart rate spiking. This is a true story.

If that does not demonstrate the versatility of an online business, I do not know what does!

Can you imagine any business model that is simpler and easier to build? If this model can be run from a hospital bed, just imagine what you can do with it.

CHAPTER 3: WHAT IS A DIGITAL PUBLISHING BUSINESS?

Here it is. The Circle of Profit. The only system you will ever need to build a ragingly successful online business!

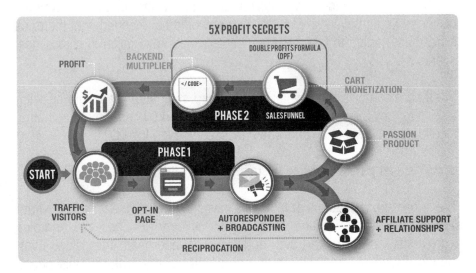

THE QUICKEST EXPLANATION

As you can see, there are many different pieces to the Circle of Profit. The rest of this book looks closely at each of those pieces.

No matter what piece we are talking about, always remember this simple diagram:

There are three major players in a digital publishing business.

- The first major player of a digital business is you.
- The second major player of a digital business is the information you have or gather.
- The third major player of a digital business is the person who is seeking information.

I like to call that last group "info seekers." The Circle of Profit connects you and your information with these info seekers. The connection of all three parts is where profit is created. This is all that a digital business is.

BUILDING SMALL CAR MODELS

Not too long ago my close friend made a very good point to me. He said, "Anik, you need a hobby. You work too much."

He was right. I needed balance in my life. I thought about it and soon remembered a childhood hobby that I used to adore.

It's called scale modeling.

You buy kits of small-scale plastic cars, planes, boats, or cities. Then you meticulously paint and construct the pieces to create a model. As a child I spent many happy hours sitting at a table building these models.

But when I got back into it years later, I had a problem. I did not remember a thing. I was starting brand new.

I forgot the skills I needed. I forgot the tools I needed. Worst of all, I forgot how to use the tools that I needed.

Guess where I turned to re-learn it all? The Internet, of course!

For days I watched dozens of videos on YouTube. I learned everything from the type of glue I needed to the right painting supplies for my kit, and much more. Then, I slowly accumulated all the best tools at the best prices.

I had to piece together every bit of information on my own from at least 50 different websites and videos. Guess what I discovered along the way?

Each video I viewed had at least 100,000 views on YouTube.

Each forum I visited had many new scale modelers asking the same questions I had. I immediately turned to my own 5-Step Checklist for Qualifying Niches (reviewed later in this book) and I found that scale modeling was the perfect example of an incredibly profitable possible niche in which to build a digital business!

I had simply set out to find a hobby that would help balance my life. I turned to a childhood passion and not only did I find my hobby, but I found an amazing niche as well – one that I am incredibly passionate about.

Guess what I am doing now?

I'm working on my first-ever 1-page website for it. I'm about to start Phase 1 of the Circle of Profit for the scale modeling niche. And I'm having a blast.

THREE BUILDING BLOCKS OF AN INFORMATION BUSINESS

The Circle of Profit uses three very simple tools to create a profitable digital publishing business around your passion.

Tool #1: Audience

Choosing a topic that has an appropriate audience with great business potential is the first key tool you need when building an information business. It is not enough that an audience is big; the audience also has to meet specific parameters. The Circle of Profit's 5-Step Checklist evaluates each potential audience. If the audience fits each of the 5 parameters, you have found a great niche. If not, I would not risk trying to force it.

For example, billions of people in the world wear underwear. Can you imagine the demand for underwear? Imagine how many people actually go to Google.com and search for underwear. The demand is there. The "audience" is there.

Despite those compelling facts, underwear is a horrible niche for digital publishing. Why? When we review the 5 Steps in the next chapter, you'll know why.

Tool #2: Email List

The next key tool you need is an email list. I will show you how to quickly build one in Phase 1 of the Circle of Profit system. There are two major benefits to having an email list:

1. You get instant access to an audience that's fully in your control.
2. You can easily build a relationship and a real trust, both consistently powerful tools for increasing your income.

To be successful, a business must be self-reliant and able to run on its own strength. Building your email list provides exactly that sustainability, and no one can ever take it away from you.

When you have a list of email subscribers, you can generate income any time. An email list empowers you to be able to create income quickly. This is because you can earn sizable commissions marketing other people's information product rather than having to wait until you've completed your own information product.

What's more, an email list can create a remarkably trusting relationship with your market. The more you email your subscribers, the more they get to know and trust you.

Tool #3: Information Products

The last key tool brings our focus face-to-face with profits. The more information products you create, the larger you can scale your business.

Why? Because when you create your own products, you get to keep the full margins on your sales. That's 100% profit. In addition, the more products you have, the more marketing channels you can use.

Information products not only help to increase your brand's value, but they substantially add income to your business.

These three building blocks - Audience, Emails, and Info - are the focus of the Circle of Profit. It doesn't get any simpler than that.

THE THREE BUILDING BLOCKS IN ACTION

Here's an example of how I personally cashed in on one of my passions.

Since I was a child, I have always been intrigued by the way the human mind works. I remember studying neuroscience in my free time as a young student. I was fascinated with how humans create emotion, and how people are so similar, yet so different.

My research led me to the study of success.

I wanted to learn what separates the über wealthy people in this world from those who seem to consistently fail - even though they have the very same opportunities. Every week I used to read new books on the topic. I even read scientific journals.

All this time I spent researching and learning gave me a unique edge on this topic. I had become very knowledgeable - almost an expert. One day I had a thought: Maybe my knowledge of neuroscience and psychology had profit potential. I knew there had to be many people in the world who shared the same passion as me. I turned to my 5 Steps to see if the topic had potential.

Lo and behold, it looked very promising. So here's what I did:

I put up a one-page website where I simply gave away a free report in exchange for my visitors to give me their email address. This was the beginning of Phase 1. I would now slowly start communicating with these subscribers and sharing my perspective and my knowledge.

Every time I read a new book or a new article, I would simply teach them what I learned. I knew that in time, I would gain a lot of trust with my audience. I also knew that over time, I would find a good deal of related educational programs that I could endorse. If my endorsement could lead me to earn a hefty commission and income, then we had a win-win!

Within just a few months, I had built an email list of over 30,000 subscribers. I was developing an incredible relationship with them and my income was scaling larger every month simply by endorsing other products.

The final peg in my master plan was to collect my research, compile my findings, and put them into my own course. So that's what I did.

Guess what?

Within six months from the first day that I had put up my 1 page test website, my new information product had created over $1 million in sales.

Today, I am considered one of the most sought-after experts in that field. And that "little" business continues to grow.

Take a look at the Circle of Profit diagram again. Notice how every part of this diagram can be grouped into any of the three building block tools.

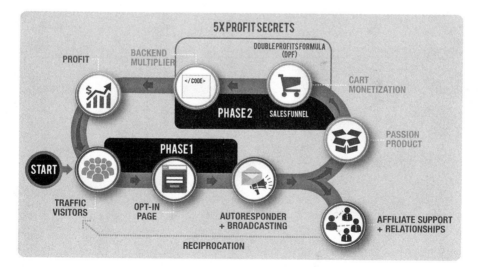

THE TWO PHASES OF MONETIZING INFORMATION

As you can see, there are two phases to the Circle of Profit. Phase 1 is all about building up your email list. Phase 2 is about creating and promoting your own information products, or "digital publishing."
Even if you stop at Phase 1, you can make great profits. But if you want to turn your passion into a million dollar empire, you need to master Phase 2 as well.

No matter what phase appeals to you or how big you want to grow your business, it all begins with one step:

Choosing your profitable topic.

The 5 Steps I've developed let you zero in on your own profitable topics and audiences. Combined, they are all you need to guarantee that you'll find a topic that inspires passion in you and that also gives you a lucrative full-time income.

CHAPTER 4: FINDING YOUR PROFITABLE PASSION

There is nothing more liberating than doing what you love. It breaks my heart when I meet people every day who absolutely despise their careers. Even worse than that is when I meet people who are considered incredibly successful, but who, deep down, are completely miserable. They are trapped in their careers because of the money they make, but they are riddled with stress and unhappiness because they lack passion.

Immersing yourself in your passion is the number one way to live a truly free and fulfilling life. It's easy to be happy when you are waking up every morning excited to get to work. Even if you have millions of dollars in your bank account, you're never truly free until you are living and working at something you love.

Trust me. I've been on both sides. Today, I'm blessed because I get to wake up every day and do what I love: teaching entrepreneurship. I get to go to sleep every night knowing that I helped thousands of people get closer to their dreams.

For me, there is absolutely no better way to live.

PASSION: THE KEY TO YOUR SUCCESS

Of course, to create a passion business, you need to know what inspires passion in you. It doesn't matter what it is. You can build your business around just about any passion.

Personally, my passion is entrepreneurship. I love giving people the tools to make their dreams a reality. To this day, there is nothing that brings a bigger smile to my face than when I get an email from a student. I often get emails that tell me how different their lives are now, and how they are living the life of their dreams - all because they applied the teachings of the Circle of Profit.

When I first started my business, my focus had always been on immersing and surrounding myself with entrepreneurship. Looking back, I think doing that was a major reason for my amazing growth. I was able to take $100 and turn it into millions even when I had no experience or prior knowledge. I loved what I was doing and I was truly passionate about every moment of my life.

But as I mentioned earlier, even after years of incredible success with the Circle of Profit business system, I began to feel that maybe it was too simple. I wanted to grow even faster. I wanted to build a company even bigger. To do that, I made the wrong assumptions, convincing myself that I needed a more complicated business model. My solution was to start building new offices, hiring a bigger team, and starting to seek investors.

These were all bad decisions that did nothing but take me away from my passion.

Before I knew it, my days were spent dealing with squabbles between employees. Or I'd spend an entire day running financial calculations trying to make ridiculous financial projections. I had gone from my passion - working with entrepreneurs - to being either an accountant or a peer mediator.

Needless to say, I began to hate my life. Even more, I began to hate my business. I woke up every morning dreading the day. My business, my team, my products, and even my customers all suddenly became a burden to me.

Believe me. Passion truly is your key to success.

We already know what kind of mental and physical damage you can do to yourself when you turn away from your passion. But it's important for you to also understand how you can recover, almost magically, simply by turning your focus back to your passion.

Even though I had fallen $1.7 million into debt, and I was nearly bankrupt and literally lying on my deathbed, it only took a tiny move to instantly bring me back to life. The night that I sat in my empty dark office and made the decision to return to the basics of the Circle of Profit model was the night I returned to my passion.

That simple decision had a profound effect on me. Within just 16 months, I had paid back every dollar of debt. Beyond that, my business was back on a steep upward trajectory to generating $10 million a year.

Passion is important. But is passion alone enough to build a strong business? What if your passion is going to the lake and skipping rocks? Is it viable to build a business on that topic? Unfortunately, the answer is no.

Once you have a list of what inspires passion in you, you must put it up against the "business test." You must make sure that you choose the passion that has the most potential commercial value in order to profit the most.

Choosing the right topic to launch a business was one of the first lessons I ever learned about 13 years ago.

And of course, I learned that lesson the hard way.

HOW I WASTED SEVEN MONTHS OF MY LIFE

When I first started learning how to make money online, I was in a rush. Thirteen years ago, there wasn't any structured training course or business system like the Circle of Profit.

I had to do it on my own.

But I wanted fast money, so I convinced myself that I didn't have time to learn or seek advice. I rushed it. I watched what I thought others were doing and I made a lot of mistaken assumptions about their business methods.

My bad assumptions and my rushed effort caused me to lose seven months of my life (and to waste the meager $100 I had to my name.)

In those days, I was obsessed with the online entrepreneur forum members who were all earning $10,000, $20,000, and even $30,000 a month. All they seemed to be doing was publishing information products and driving visitors to a web page.

It looked so simple! Surely I could do it even better.

Not so much.

I assumed that any niche would work. As long as there were a lot of people in that niche and they had money, I assumed I was good to go. Back then, I only had two steps to review a niche. But I soon learned that those two steps were simply not enough.

Here's what happened: For years, I had been really good at finding ways to ace my college exams without studying. I knew there were millions of college students. College students who spent tens of thousands of dollars on their education.

So this niche made all kinds of sense to me. I saw a sizable audience with access to a lot of money. I thought, "Wow, I must be onto something."

What excited me even more was that I could not find a single competitor in the entire market! I thought I had struck gold. I was convinced I would be a millionaire before college was even over.

But the product was a complete flop.

I spent seven months of my life barking up the wrong tree. I had never taken the time to truly understand the difference between a passion and a profitable passion.

Luckily, you don't have to make the same mistake. Let's dive in.

IS YOUR PASSION PROFITABLE?

So what kind of passion is profitable and capable of generating $1 million?

To find out, your topic must satisfy each of the following five checklist points. If you ignore these five points, or pretend that your niche fits them when it doesn't, you're only setting yourself up for failure.

We're going to cover the following 5 Niche Research Metrics in more detail in Chapter 14. For now, get familiar with these ideas and qualification methods:

1. Digital Information Friendly
This one is easy. You can determine the answer in less than 20 seconds. Digital friendly means the ability to take the topic and monetize digital products - information, software, or apps - for it. The end product has to be something that is purchased and delivered digitally.

Here are a few examples:

- Underwear. Is this digital friendly or not? Nope. No matter how hard you try, it's impossible to download underwear.
- Weight Loss. Yes, this is absolutely digital information friendly; you can easily sell information about weight loss and deliver it digitally.
- Brake Pads for a Car. Not really. However, if you broaden your topic into car care or car modification, this topic starts to get digital-friendly.
- How to Invest in Stocks. Yes. This is a fantastic example of a digital product-friendly niche market.

That was the easy part. Next, we have to start using tools and doing more thorough research.

2. Competition
When it comes to competition, here is one simple (but surprising) rule: Never be the first to release a digital product in a niche in which no one else is already selling a digital product.

Remember how my very first product was information on how to ace exams in college? One of the reasons I got most excited about that niche idea was because there was absolutely no competition in the market!

This is a common mistake that many digital publishers make when they are starting out. At first, it feels like common sense to choose a niche with no competition. But in practice, you'll find this is the complete opposite of the reality.

In the beginning, it's smartest to go into a proven market where you can emulate a proven model. That leads us to the final question: How do you find out whether or not others are selling online education in your niche market?

Simple. Go to the following three sources and put your niche keywords into their search tool. You can complete this research in thirty minutes or less.

1. Clickbank.com
Clickbank.com is a digital marketplace built to help digital publishers sell courses in a wide array of niches. From weight loss to surviving the end of the world to southern cooking recipes, Clickbank has it all.

2. Udemy.com
Udemy is the new industry leader in online education and online courses. It started just a few years ago and has gone on to put together over 20,000 online courses! It allows anyone from anywhere in the world to become their own digital publishing house.

Use Udemy's search tool to check whether others are offering education in your chosen niche. Udemy even tells you how many customers are signed up for a particular course, so you can also check to see how well the courses in your niche are actually selling.

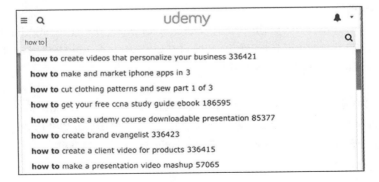

3. Google.com

If Clickbank and Udemy provide you with no results (or mixed results), here's how to use Google: Just search for courses in your niche. However, I usually find that if Clickbank and Udemy do not already have the courses I'm seeking, Google rarely reverses that verdict.

The bottom line? Do not try to create new markets. Keep it simple and only pursue the niches in which others are already selling similar products. Always remember that competition means potential; it is unsurpassed in providing a realistic proof point for a market - and it almost completely eliminates your risk.

3. Size of Audience

This is where we start to have fun using free tools that are available on the Internet. The tools I will show you are not necessarily created for the purpose that we are using them. But they work incredibly well and they're absolutely free!

One of the parameters I use to evaluate a digital publishing business is a 1 million person market. If I find that a market is less than 1 million people, I feel the scale is very limited.

Often, the smaller the market, the harder it is to drive traffic. That's because there is usually less overall activity, and that can make it much more difficult for you to break into that space.

Sticking to a minimum 1 million person market size helps me get around this obstacle. But how do we determine the size of a market? With Facebook Advertising!

Don't worry. You are not going to spend a dime in advertising. So why Facebook Advertising? Because it offers an excellent analytics tool called Audience Insights.

This tool gives you useful information in about 2 minutes. Simply choose the countries on which you want to focus. I recommend the United States, Canada, Australia, New Zealand, the United Kingdom, France, and Germany. These countries will give you the best idea about the size of your "active market."

Next, enter keywords that describe your niche. Do not type in keywords that describe your product; you want to see your niche size - not your product size. For instance, let's say you have some amazing tips on how to scrapbook. Do not type in keywords like "scrapbook templates." That term is describing your product.

Instead, enter keywords like "scrapbooking." This will give you an idea of just how many people in the world are interested in the topic of scrapbooking.

As you can see, Facebook tells us that 6,187,530 people are interested in the scrapbooking niche. Since we're seeing more than 1 million people, it looks like this part of the research process checks out.

This tool is free, simple, and very fast - and it will save you an incredible number of headaches. Use it.

4. Popularity in Search

Let's start learning some more about your niche. Let's assume that we feel confident that there is a sizable number of people in your market.

How can we now determine whether these people are actually interested in your solution?

And do they have any specific pain points that you can resolve?

This time we are going to turn to Google's Keyword Planner Tool.

Once you pull this tool up, all you need to do is type in keywords that you believe your market would enter to find your product on Google. There is no perfect way of doing this, so just take an hour and try a variety of keywords and keyword combinations.

Because I do not know your topic or keywords, it is hard to give you a specific number of searches that you should seek. However, for the main keywords that you choose, there should be at least 10,000 searches per month. It's ideal if there are even more.

In some niches, people use a lot of different keywords for their searches. In these cases, each individual keyword may not give you a result of 10,000. But when you add up the search numbers of the main keywords, you can often end up with a very strong overall search number.

Now go and see if your market is interested in your potential information product.

5. Long Term Potential

How long will your customer be interested in buying your education products? Here's an example: One of my students is a pediatric nurse. She wanted to launch a business in the niche of "infant teething."

On the face of it, it sounded like an amazing niche. There are countless new mothers in this world, right? Almost every new mother asks hundreds of questions about how to care for her child, and she usually reads many books on the subject.

If I had to make a hasty decision, I would have said that this niche sounded promising.

But then I thought about the span of time that a mother would be interested in information about teething.

The long term potential for infant teething education products is very small.

Why? Because within a couple of days, that mother will have the information she wanted - and she'll have no need for your information anymore.

Now compare this to the niche of golfing. A golfer today will most likely still be a golfer three years from now. Golfing isn't a problem that you can solve after 3 days of research. In other words, if golfers are buying golfing education today, they'll probably still be interested in buying more on an ongoing basis - and for years to come!

Having a niche that offers this kind of ongoing, long term potential is what makes the biggest difference in your continued ability to scale larger. Although it is Step 5 in this checklist, it is one of the steps I think the most about.

PASSIONS THAT ARE VERY PROFITABLE

To help you get going with some ideas, here's a starting point.

The best topics for launching an online business tend to be in the Big 3:

1. Health (Physical, Spiritual, and Emotional)
2. Wealth (Business, Investing, etc.)
3. Relationships (Marriage, Dating, Parenting, etc.)

These are NOT the only three. There are plenty of other niches. But in my career, I have seen the bulk of great success come from these three areas.

Here are some more examples to get you thinking:

- Weight Loss, Bodybuilding, Healthy Eating, Superfoods
- Dating Advice, Divorce
- Real Estate, Investing
- Electronics/Gadgets, Gaming
- Pets
- Finding a Job
- Panic Attacks, Reiki, Hypnosis

To sum up: As long as you have passion, an active market with money, long term potential, and existing competition, you can turn any viable topic into $1 million using the Circle of Profit.

Now that we have the niche selection process out of the way, there is only one thing left to do: It is time to start building your business.

SECTION 2: YOUR INFORMATION EMPIRE

CHAPTER 5: YOUR CRASH COURSE TO THE CIRCLE OF PROFIT

In this chapter, I'm going to give you a bird's-eye view of the Circle of Profit.

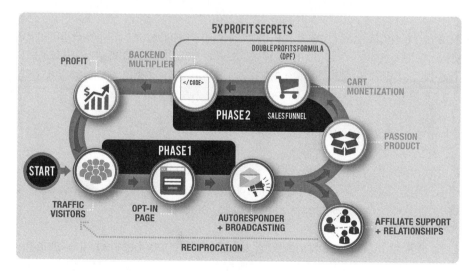

Phase 1 is all about building an audience of fans; subscribers who trust you and look to you as an expert and a qualified source of information. During this phase, you will grow your email reach by getting more and more people to give you their email address. You will also nurture relationships with your new subscribers.

Most of all, you will start generating a healthy profit from these new subscribers. In this way, your business can be profitable from day one.

Phase 2 is about creating $1 million. We monetize your newfound influence to the next level by creating and promoting your own information products. These may include eBooks, audios, videos, or a combination.

This is where your profits are really going to explode.

It really is as straightforward as that.
1. Use the system to get visitors to your website.
2. Get them to give you their email address.
3. Provide these new subscribers with something they value.
4. Keep them happy.
5. Present to them the ability to buy great information products.
6. Create profit.
7. Rinse and repeat.

The more profit you create, the more you can reinvest to drive even more visitors to your site. The more visitors you get, the bigger your email list. The bigger your email list, the more sales you get. The more sales you get, the more profits you make. Do you see how this works now?

It forms a circle: The Circle of Profit.

In the next chapter, I'm going to give you an overview of the key elements of each phase. You'll see that this model is not complicated. It just comes down to following the steps and providing value.

Let's look at the key elements you'll need to start your business the fastest.

CHAPTER 6: THE KEY ELEMENTS TO STARTING YOUR BUSINESS

PHASE 1: MAKING YOUR FIRST PROFIT

As you already know, Phase 1 is all about email marketing. Here I am going to teach you how to start creating a profit by promoting products that already exist. You do not need to create anything new. All you need to do is send emails, which endorse existing products, to your new subscribers.

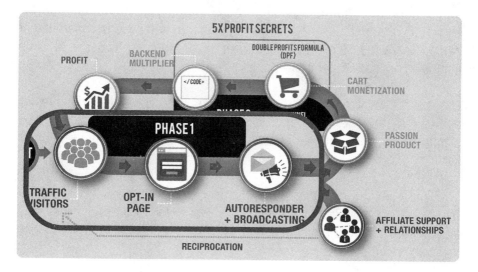

Using nothing but a simple "affiliate link," you will begin to generate commissions (your percentage share of a sale) that can be as high as 75%. That's right. You can actually earn more than the person who owns the product.

WHAT IS A SUBSCRIBER WORTH?

Let's say you're in the business of teaching people how to invest in the stock market. Maybe you've been able to use your investing strategies to completely change your life, and now you want to help others to do the same.

Following the Phase 1 model, you begin to attract visitors to your one page website and they start to share their email addresses with you.

An email address (if treated properly) is worth a lot of money. It is a true business asset. A value very commonly accepted by information marketing experts is $1 per email address.

That means that if you can build an email list of 10,000 subscribers, you can generate a profit of $10,000 per month - simply by properly managing that list!

Of course, that number is not written in stone. In some niches, the number can be as low as 50 cents per email per month. In other niches, that value can be as high as $5 per email per month.

But the great thing about Phase 1 and knowing the value of an email address is that it lets you stop focusing on making money. Instead, you simply focus on the number of subscribers you have in your growing email list.

The longer you are a marketer, the better you get at it. The bigger your list, the better opportunities that come your way. Not to mention when you launch Phase 2, your profit margins go up. Your profits begin to grow along with your value per lead per month!

To quickly understand just how an email address is worth money to you, we're going to need some math. To make the math easy, use the $1 per lead per month value.

INSIDE THE CIRCLE: VIDEO BREAK #2

KEY HOOK: See What My Subscribers Are Worth To My List
Go Here To Watch This Free Video:
www.lurn.com/blog/KeyHook

Ready to do some math?

HOW DOES AN EMAIL LIST TRANSLATE INTO PROFITS?

For this exercise to make sense, we have to make one key assumption: That you have built an email list of 10,000 subscribers.

This is only an example. Every number in our calculations can (and very likely will) change based on your list and your individual emails.

Let's say you send an email to your 10,000 subscribers. In the email, you endorse a product as an affiliate. That simply means that someone else owns the product, and in your email you insert a unique link that brings your subscribers to the product owner's site.

Now, whenever a sale happens, you get a commission - as high as 75%.

INSIDE THE CIRCLE: VIDEO BREAK #3

How An Email Turns Into Profit
Find Out Now! Watch This Free Video:
www.lurn.com/blog/email

You should be able to get between 2% and 7% of your subscribers to click the link in your email. To keep the math simple, let's assume 5% of your 10,000 subscribers click the link.

5% x 10,000 subscribers = 500 clicks.

If the sales page is well done, you can typically get a 2% conversion rate. A 2% conversion rate means that 2% of the people who clicked will buy the product.

Again, remember that these numbers will vary depending on the specifics of the promotion, list, sales page, etc. Some are better, and some are worse. In this example, we're using broad digital marketing industry averages.

Two percent of 500 clicks works out to 10 sales (2% x 500 clicks = 10 sales). Now, let's assume the product costs $97 and you get 75% commission.

On this promotion, you would generate 10 sales x $97 = $970 in sales.

At 75% commission, with just one email on one day, you would have earned $970 x 75% = $727.50.

That's over $700 in pure profit just for taking five minutes to write and send one email!

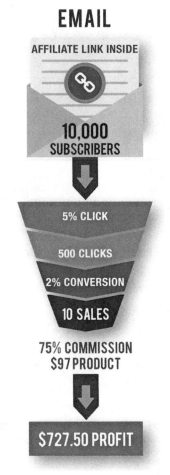

Even if you only made half of that, you'd still be earning more than $10,000 a month.

NOTE: I want to once again emphasize that this is not a guarantee and a lot of factors can change these numbers. I do, however, want you to see the huge potential in all of this.

Now you can understand mathematically that Phase 1 (Building Your Email List) is incredibly important and profitable at the same time. For Phase 1, here are the 3 parts you need to focus on:
Part 1. Traffic
Part 2. Your opt-in page
Part 3. Your autoresponder

Let's break each of these down in detail.

PHASE 1, PART 1: TRAFFIC

We'll start with another quick example.

Let's say you open up a physical store near your house. Your store will never make any money unless people walk in, right?

The same thing applies to your online business. You have to get visitors to your website in order to stand a chance at making a profit. We call the process of getting visitors: traffic acquisition.

Do you know the saying, "If you build it, they will come?" This is absolutely not true when it comes to your online business.

There are billions of pages on the Internet. Most of them get absolutely no visitors - not even one. The irony is that getting traffic to your website is actually not hard at all. There is a list of simple steps to follow, and all you need to do is copy and paste these steps.

And miraculously, getting traffic to your website is easy, fast, and inexpensive.

You do not have to spend thousands of dollars. You are not risking your life's savings by having to buy an expensive TV commercial. And you don't have to spend weeks waiting for a billboard to be put up.

As a matter of fact, on the Internet, you can start with as little as $50 (or even free) and see your first profitable traffic in as little as 30 minutes.

In Chapter 10 I'm going to break down proven traffic-generating strategies that lead to immediate profit. There is something to fit any budget that you can afford - even if your budget is $0.

Just look at all the options you have. It's amazing:

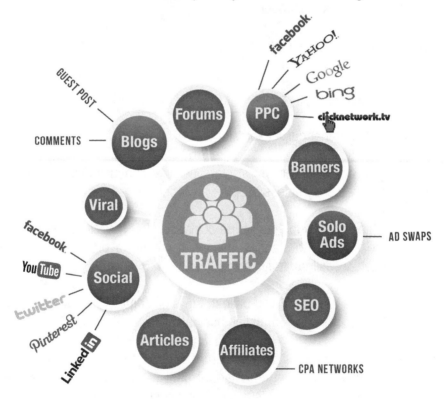

PHASE 1, PART 2: YOUR OPT-IN PAGE

Let's go back to the example of building a store.

Obviously, if you go out and rent land, you will need to build the store, right? You will need shelves, desks, chairs, inventory, signs, lights, and more. This can end up costing you tens of thousands of dollars, if not more.

Online, you still need a place for people to go. There's just one big difference: You don't need thousands of dollars. You don't even need hundreds of dollars.

All you need to start turning your passion into pure profit is a one page website. That's it. We call these websites opt-in pages. You'll see why in just a minute.

The most amazing part is that an opt-in page can be created without any technical experience. You never have to program or write any code. All you have to do is click a few buttons using our automated system.

You never sell anything on these websites. Remember, at this point, you don't even have your own product. Opt-in pages have only one purpose: To convince your site visitor to give you his or her email address and subscribe to your email list.

The great news is that in over 13 years of testing, I have found that the simpler your opt-in pages, the higher your conversion rates. If you try to get fancy and complicated, your conversions actually drop.

This is great news for you. This means that it's easier than ever to start generating profits using Phase 1 of the Circle of Profit.

Now, when I say simple, what exactly do I mean? Look at the example below. This page was created using our own click-click technology. It probably took about 7 minutes to create.

That's it. That's how simple an opt-in page is. All we did to create it was write the headline (the large bold words at the top). We chose some standard images that the system placed at the top and bottom. Then, we plugged in the name of the autoresponder that we created at SendLane.com (which the system does for you automatically).

Voilá – we're in business!

HOW I GOT 3,640 SUBSCRIBERS IN THREE DAYS USING THIS OPT-IN PAGE

I sent over 7,000 clicks to this opt-in page from various sources of traffic. My overall average conversion was 52%!

That means that of the 7,000 visitors who came to this page, 52% of them gave me their email address.

That page took me just minutes to build. And in just three days, I was able to build an email list of over 3,640. I was in business and generating a very healthy profit.

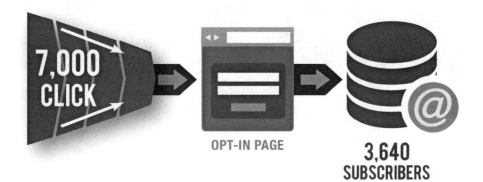

How many businesses do you know that can launch and profit that fast?

PHASE 1, PART 3: THE AUTORESPONDER

The email addresses you collect on your opt-in page do not sit on your own computer. They actually fly into a database automatically, using a copy-and-paste line of code that you've put on your page. This database of email addresses is called an autoresponder.

There are many third party companies, which will manage the entire autoresponder process for you. It's incredibly easy. They give you a line of code that you simply copy and paste into your opt-in page. Instantly, the email addresses that your visitors enter are automatically placed into your autoresponder.

I recommend SendLane.com. You can even get a Free 30 Trial account by going here: www.lurn.com/FreeSendLaneTrial

There are two major benefits of having an autoresponder:

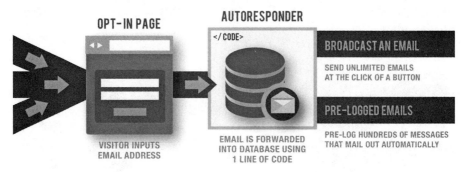

1. You can send thousands of emails in seconds.

You simply type out an email message once (just as you would to a friend) and hit "send." Instantly, the autoresponder system sends it to thousands of email addresses. The power of an autoresponder is that you can email everyone with just one click. The system handles the rest!

2. You can pre-log hundreds of messages ahead of time.

Talk about automation! With an autoresponder, you can pre-log as many emails as you want and the system will start sending your new subscribers daily emails, all on its own. The system automatically remembers which subscriber joined your list and on which day. According to their day, thousands of different subscribers can be getting thousands of different pre-logged emails everyday, in the proper order and at the right time of day.

In Chapter 8, I'm going to break down the secrets of how to use an autoresponder for maximum profits. I will show you three types of emails that automate the entire process.

Now that we've covered our quick introduction to Phase 1, we're ready to move to Phase 2.

This is a very important phase for your business. This is when we start to talk about building true empires. If your dream is to have a million dollar business, then Phase 2 of the Circle of Profit is a must.

PHASE 2: THE SECRET TO CREATING $1 MILLION

Phase 2 is all about turning your passion into $1 million. The best and fastest way to do this is by creating and promoting your own digital content products. If you follow the steps of Phase 2 properly, you're going to see serious growth and fast profits. The secrets of this phase took my business from about $300,000 a year to over $10 million a year.

The 2 key elements to creating your first $1 million using Phase 2 are:

1. Your Passion Product
2. Your $1 Million Funnel

Let me introduce you to both.

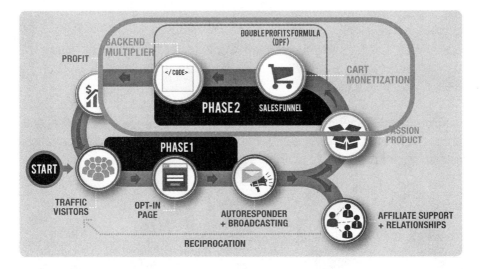

YOUR PASSION PRODUCT

As long as you have access to information that can help others who share your passion (even if you simply collect that information and put it into one place), you have what it takes to create a very successful information product.

If you want to teach fitness, you don't need to be a certified trainer or nutritionist. Your credibility can come from many places. Perhaps you've lost a lot of weight yourself. Perhaps you partner with a friend who has the related certifications. There are endless possibilities!

Remember that the whole magic of the Circle of Profit is that it allows you to build your business with a very small budget.

YOUR $1 MILLION FUNNEL

What I'm about to tell you took me at least three years to learn. However, when I finally learned it, I became unstoppable. To really take your profits to the next level, you will hear me use this term many times: Funnel.

A funnel is a group of products that are strategically sold, one by one, to existing customers.

For example, let's say you go to McDonald's and order a Big Mac. The cashier behind the register asks, "Do you want fries with that?" Then he asks if you'd like a soda, too.

You were just the target of a small sales funnel: After you agree to become a customer by asking for a Big Mac, the company positions other beneficial and complementary offers in front of you.

By adding french fries and a soda to your order (simply by asking you), McDonald's just doubled the size of your order. Multiply that by millions of daily Big Mac eaters, and just imagine what that funnel does to their revenue.

In short, the goal of a funnel is to convince an existing customer to buy more products from the company increasing the lifetime customer value - and profits, of course.

This is a concept that absolutely changed my life. In later chapters, I will show you actual examples of funnels for a digital product online business.

PHASES 1 AND 2: COMPLETING THE CIRCLE

The true power of the Circle of Profit lies in using Phase 1 and Phase 2 together. When built properly, the entire system can be automated using the Circle of Profit.

Always remember that:
Phase 1 builds your business foundation with these crucial elements:

1. Start building your email list.
2. Begin creating a fast profit from your business.
3. Build a strong relationship with your subscribers.

Phase 2 puts you on the road to generating really big profits:

1. Build scale into your business.
2. Generate profits that go into the millions.
3. Be able to reinvest those profits.

The more each phase grows, the more your profits skyrocket.

Now it's time to start peeling back all the layers. You've learned the basics of each phase, so let's get into the details of Phase 1.

It's time to rock and roll!

CHAPTER 7: BUILDING YOUR AUDIENCE

Phase 1 of the Circle of Profit is all about building an audience of fans. The larger your audience, the more sales you make. The more passionate they are about you and your message, the more sales you make. The more sales you make, the more you can afford to grow your audience by reinvesting in more traffic.

In order to get new fans to opt-in to your email list, you need to direct them to your opt-in page. This is where you basically offer them something free in exchange for their email address.

Making your opt-in page is very easy. It just takes a few clicks. The best part is that the simpler your opt-in page, the better your conversions will be.

Remember this example?

This simple page took me a total of seven minutes to create. It converts at over 52%. With this page, I was able to launch a business in the fitness niche in less than one day. The entire key to this business is this opt-in page.

Without an opt-in page, you have no business. So let's learn the details of an opt-in page.

A high conversion opt-in page must include these three key elements:

1. The Headline
2. The Free Gift
3. The Opt-In Box

Let's look more closely at each one.

1. The Headline

The headline is the most important component of your opt-in page. It's the first and most prominent thing your visitor sees when landing on your opt-in page. No opt-in page will ever work without a very strong headline.

Just look at my opt-in page sample. The headline is big, bold, and has a very convincing promise.

Within seconds of seeing this page, you get a very strong and intriguing promise. You are being enticed to get free information on how to lose 10% of your body fat in just 30 days.

Think about it: If you're someone looking to lose weight, this headline will catch your attention almost instantly. That's why this page can convert at 52%.

Years of testing has proven that the number one element of a high-conversion opt-in page is a strong headline. You can make your graphics as pretty as you want, but the results of pretty graphics do not come close to the results you get with even a small improvement to the headline.

When someone comes to your opt-in page, you only have a few seconds to grab them. Your headline must be the main thing they read - and the promise must be strong enough to stop them in their tracks.

2. The Free Gift

Decades of research has proven repeatedly that the most powerful word in marketing is "free."

It doesn't even matter what you're giving away. If it's free, people will line up around the block to get it! No question about it: The one word that is most responsible for my $10 million a year passion business is the word "free."

To get someone to give you his or her email address, you have to be willing to offer something in return. Rarely will anyone want to give you something as personal as their email address without getting something in return. Because of this, we simply use an opt-in page to offer a small - completely legal - bribe.

We offer people amazing information for free in exchange for their email address. In this example, we are offering to give them a free report. This report could be a 10 to 20 page PDF file that takes very little time to create. However, it's an incredibly powerful way to convince someone to give you his or her email address.

3. The Opt-In Box

The final key component of your opt-in page is a little box in which your visitor enters his or her email address. This box is the easiest part of your opt-in page. You simply copy and paste the line of code provided to you by your autoresponder.

It's so easy, you might even forget it. But beware: Without this box, the visitor's email address will never make it to your database. It's so important that I always add some reinforcing text to all of my opt-in boxes. For instance, I'll emphasize the free offer again to make sure I close the deal.

Here's an example:

As I mentioned previously, you can create your opt-in box very easily. You simply copy and paste a line of code given to you by your autoresponder company.

HOW TO CAPTURE 10,113 EMAILS IN 45 DAYS

This is an opt-in page example in the Personal Development space. More specifically, it's in the Law of Attraction niche. The page was designed using a simple template. The entire page took our student less than 60 minutes to create.

In this example, the student chose to invest about $60 with an outsourcer using the same techniques that I teach, and the entire process was automated. The student never touched any technology.

After the page went live on the student's domain name, she took another two days to create her free gift. This free gift was positioned as a short course that could be downloaded in PDF format. The entire PDF was only 40 pages, but each page had valuable content for the reader. The free gift PDF was also outsourced for an investment of only $150.

So in less than three days, this student had her opt-in page and her free course completely done for only $210.

For just $210, this student had taken her passion for the Law of Attraction and converted it into a lifelong business that will be full of profits.

After the opt-in page and the free gift were live online, our student began to generate traffic using two specific techniques that we teach.

1. She used free traffic.
2. She used email media (which requires a small investment).

The results? This student generated more than 22,473 visitors to this one simple page. The page converted at 45% of these, resulting in more than 10,113 subscribers. The student made her very first profit within seven days.

Today she is generating over $6,000 a month in income.

This income allowed the student to quit her day job. Now she is 100% focused on her passion business, and plans to launch her own passion product any day now. The minute her product launches, she expects to immediately see her income jump from $6,000 a month to over $15,000 a month.

Behold the power of the simple, yet intelligently created, opt-in page!

Here's another example:

MAKING $14,955 IN THE FIRST 30 DAYS

This student chose to focus on the power of affiliate marketing.

This opt-in page is about as simple as it gets. It was built in 5 minutes using the free landing page builder at SendLane - 100% with automated technology that cost the student nothing.

Investment in opt-in page = $0
The free gift on this page is an audio recording the student produced himself. He used a microphone and his laptop. He outlined the audio course in about two hours and then recorded it in another two hours.

The free gift was done in four hours, and went live immediately after that.

Investment in free gift = $0
In one day, this student had a live business, ready to go.

Next, the student chose to use only one source of traffic. This traffic source is 100% free. He invested absolutely no money into traffic and built a list of 5,450 within the first 30 days.

Investment in traffic = $0
I want to mention here that the student spent about four hours a day on

traffic generation strategies because he did not want to invest even a small amount of money into traffic. This is absolutely fine. Just remember, if you don't invest money, you need to be ready to invest time.

$14,955 in the first 30 days
25 days into building this email list, this student had a chance to promote a very strong affiliate product offering very high commissions. The product cost $997 and the commission was 50%. That meant that the student would earn $498.50 per sale.

Using some very specific promotional techniques, the student was able to sell 30 units of this $997 product - before his business was even 30 days old. At his 50% commission level, he had now earned $14,955 in his first 30 days.

These are the kind of results we hear about all the time. This student has already begun working on his passion product and I expect he will see his income multiply in the next 30 to 45 days. Amazing, isn't it?

I could go on for hours with more examples and case studies. The fact is, this system works. The key is to simply put it into action and be patient. As long as you focus on driving traffic to your one page website, it is nearly impossible for you not to make money.

Now that you understand how simple opt-in pages are, let's move on to the next necessary step. You need to learn how to build a trusting, enthusiastic relationship with your new audience.

CHAPTER 8: TALKING TO YOUR AUDIENCE

With the help of your new opt-in page, you should have new email list subscribers flying in. But it takes more than that to start making a profit. We want your subscribers to become raving fans who look to you as an authority on your topic - and take you seriously enough to make purchasing decisions based on your advice.

This is where the profits come in!

To turn subscribers into fans, you need to communicate with them. That means you need to send them emails.

This is precisely where your email autoresponder comes in.

The invention of the autoresponder revolutionized online marketing. It automates everything involved with setting up and maintaining your email list. With an autoresponder, you can send emails to your audience in two ways:

1. Pre-logged emails, which are based on the date a subscriber joins your list.
2. Broadcast emails, which are sent to all of your subscribers at once.

Pre-logged emails. When you use pre-logged emails, you can schedule emails ahead of time and the autoresponder automatically sends them to your subscribers.

For example, you can assign a welcome email (which you need to only type once in your life) to go out immediately after the subscriber joins. The next one can be scheduled for one day after the subscriber joined. The next one two days after. You get the picture. There are no limits; you can schedule pre-logged emails out for 10 years if you want.

CAPTURE EMAIL ADDRESS	EMAIL ADDRESS STORED	DAY 0 - IMMEDIATE EMAIL SENT	*FOLLOW-UP EMAILS SENT DAILY (1-10)

Broadcast emails. When using the broadcasting feature, you simply log in to your autoresponder. You type up your email (there are three types of emails, which we'll discuss in the next section) and you hit send. It doesn't matter if you have 500 subscribers or 50,000; that's all you do. Every person on your list will receive that email.

CAPTURE EMAIL ADDRESS	EMAIL ADDRESS STORED	DAY 0 - IMMEDIATE EMAIL SENT	SEND LIVE EMAIL BROADCAST

I would say that 95% of my own wealth has been generated using the broadcast feature. I use pre-logged emails for a very specific reason (discussed in the next section). After that I turn my full focus to broadcast emails.

Obviously, every autoresponder is different, each with different features. Your ability to profit from your email list, then, depends on what features you are provided. Let's discuss the most common autoresponders in the market. I'll also share a secret with you that has been building for 18 months.

AUTORESPONDERS: WHICH ONE TO CHOOSE?

An autoresponder is a critical tool in your online business. It is also very difficult to switch once you are committed to one, so make your choice wisely, right from the start.

Full disclosure: I am a co-founder of an autoresponder company. I have helped guide the company in its development, features, marketing, and vision.

Of course, my recommendation of this company will seem biased. But I am personally one of the happiest customers of my own company. My partners and I built this autoresponder company out of sheer need. There are other great autoresponders in the world. But none of them cater specifically to digital publishers like you.

The name of the autoresponder I recommend most is SendLane.com. If you are looking for an autoresponder, I highly recommend you go to: www.Lurn.com/sendlane.

We will even give you 30 days free because you invested in the Circle of Profit!

Is SendLane the only good option? Not at all. There are three others that I can personally vouch for:

1. GetResponse
2. iContact
3. Aweber

These are the three most popular simply because of the features they offer, their pricing, and their frequency of use among the online business crowd. None will truly match the features, focus, and pricing of SendLane, but I want you to be aware of all your options.

Have a look at all of them and make your decision. No matter what, you will need at least one of them. You cannot build your business without an autoresponder.

HOW TO WRITE EMAILS TO YOUR SUBSCRIBERS: THREE KINDS OF EMAILS

There are three different types of emails you need to master. They can be used for both your pre-logged emails and for your broadcasting emails.

I have always found it more profitable to focus on broadcasting rather than the pre-logged autoresponder emails. I believe the reason broadcast emails work better is because they allow you to send timely, current messages using the news, industry gossip, and breakthroughs.

I do use the pre-logged emails as well. Every scenario is different, but I like to send these out during the first 10 days of a customer's subscription. They're perfect for introducing myself, and as a way for my new subscribers to get to know me.

So, once a person gives me his or her email address:

1. Day 0 - Day 10 = Pre-logged emails
2. Day 11 - Lifetime = Broadcast emails

I recommend emailing your list daily. I do, at least once a day. I have known marketers who email their list even more than that - as often as three times a day - although I believe that might be overkill.

We have consistently found that students who email their list daily are far outperforming the students who email their list only once a week.

There is a common misconception that if you email your list less frequently, they will pay more attention. This is simply not true and has been proven to be wrong many times.

THE THREE EMAILS

So, what are the three different types of emails that I recommend alternating between? If you use a combination of these three, you will build a strong relationship with your subscribers, and you will begin to profit incredibly fast.

When you write an email to your list, keep a balanced rotation of the following three types:

1. Content emails
2. Promotional emails
3. Relationship emails

Here is a brief overview of each of the three. We will get even more detailed soon:

1. Content Emails

Great content is your bread and butter. The key to making the Circle of Profit work is to give your customers a lot of value; truly helpful content. There are many ways of getting high quality content, without being particularly brilliant or a published expert in the topic.

Basically, you want your subscribers to feel like they learn something new and valuable whenever they engage with you. They should have fun with your emails. Your subscribers should be excited to open your emails - and the best way to get there is by writing Content Emails.

2. Promotional Emails

This is where the profit comes in. Typically, at least once a week, I recommend sending your subscribers an email about a product that you believe will really help improve their lives.

You can either promote your own products (discussed in the next section) or you can promote existing products as an affiliate. As an affiliate, you'll recall, you are paid a commission from sales resulting from your endorsement.

You'll do this a lot during Phase 1, which focuses on promoting products as an affiliate. In Phase 2, which focuses on adding your own products to the promotions, you'll promote your own products more.

I am a big fan of affiliate offers. The great thing about affiliate offers is that you never have to invest much time before you start generating profits.

Many affiliate commissions are as high as 75%, which means you can actually earn more than the product owners themselves.

Simply find excellent products that others have created, get your personal affiliate link, and endorse the product to your email list.

3. Relationship Emails

Who do you trust more: a friend or a stranger? The answer is obvious: Your friend. And when your email list subscribers start seeing you more as a friend than some random person sending them emails, you'll get the best response.

I like to make my subscribers feel like they're a part of my life. My best students are the ones who take the time to get personal with their list.

They will send subscribers "inside" information about their worldly travels. They share personal stories with them about major moments in their life.

Many even talk about their families. These are all things we would do with our friends. When you get personal with your email list, it automatically triggers an emotional response in the recipient's brain to regard you as a friend. After all, that's how their conversations go with their own close friends.

You see, the more personal you get with your list, the more trust you build with them. It becomes obvious to them that you have nothing to hide and that there is a real person behind that computer contacting them.

The more trust you build with your email list, the more profits you will earn.

Very shortly, I'm going to give you specific branding strategies that will allow you to get personal with your list with almost no effort and no time investment on your part.

And now, here's a funny story...

"ANIK! HOW WAS YOUR GONDOLA RIDE?"

I was recently in Las Vegas hosting a seminar. There were over 700 students there. All of these students are subscribers of mine and as I would soon learn, they are also avid readers of the emails I send out.

A little background: I was recently married. One of the places my wife and I visited on our honeymoon was Venice, Italy. While we were traveling, I decided to run some promotions for a product I truly believe in. As my bride and I climbed onto the gondola ride in Venice, I had an ingenious idea.

"Why not shoot a video while we're on this ride, and send it to my list?"

Yup. I made my poor wife hold the camera while I shot a three minute video teaching everyone about a topic I was passionate about. Obviously, I introduced the video by sharing where I was, who I was with, and what we were doing there.

Then I emailed the video to my list - and promptly forgot about it.

Weeks later I was at the seminar in Las Vegas and I heard a student chasing me down from behind: "Anik! How was your gondola ride?"

For an instant, I freaked out. How did this student know I was on a gondola in Venice? Then I quickly remembered that I had shot the video and sent it out. It didn't stop there.

During the event, I must have had at least twenty students bring up the gondola ride, and far more asking if they could meet my wife!

My students and subscribers were asking me about where I went on my honeymoon, and many other questions. The same types of questions my close friends and family asked me after the trip.

I realized that by sharing these moments with my list, I was inviting my subscribers into my life. I was making them feel as if they were a part of my circle of family and friends.

Talk about trust. That's how to build a true relationship with your list.

As we'll discuss later in this book, if you send out a nice mix of these three types of emails, you will keep your subscribers completely engaged. They will never grow blind to your emails because you will always keep it fresh.

All of this combined will make a very sizable impact on the profits you generate.

Trust me. I'm not a star writer or a talented author. And as I've already mentioned, the only class I nearly failed in high school was writing.

But with the tips and tricks you'll read about later in this book, you're going to learn how to easily become a master author in the eyes of your subscribers. All by just writing a short email.

One of the most common hurdles I see students face is the fear of promoting a product to their list. We start to build such a strong relationship with our subscribers that we fear we might lose that relationship if we promote something to them.

This couldn't be farther from the truth! Promoting or endorsing a product to your email list is one of the best ways to maintain and further build that relationship with your list.

Here's one way to look at it: What if you were at the mall and saw a huge mega sale at your favorite store? After you finished shopping, wouldn't you call or text a few of your closest friends? What if you didn't call them? Wouldn't those friends be a little miffed at you?

Better yet, think about the last time your friend saw you using something or buying a new product, and then asked you how you liked it. If you loved the product, you most likely gave a raving review about it.

The next day, that same friend may have gone out and purchased the same product. Did you feel bad? Not likely. If anything, I bet you felt great, and maybe even a little proud.

This is why promoting a product to your list is actually doing your subscribers a service. Never be too shy or feel awkward about doing it; your subscribers will love you for it.

OPEN RATES AND CLICK RATES

Let me show you a test I recently conducted on my own subscribers. I wanted to test to see what they liked more: 100% pure content or a product endorsement.

In this case, I tracked two variables:

1. Open Rate – The percentage of people on my email list who opened my email.

2. Click Rate – The percentage of people on my email list who clicked a link in my email.

The results were amazing. I found that my list was far more engaged when I was sending a product recommendation - much more than when I asked them to go to my blog to watch a free video.

I have since repeated this test three times, and each time I've gotten the same results.

Again, your Open Rate is the percentage of people who open your email. If you send an email to a list of 10,000 subscribers and 1,600 people open it, your open rate is 16%.

The Click Rate (or Click Through Rate) is the percentage of people who actually click the link that's in your email message. This number can either be calculated based on the total number of emails you sent, or you can calculate your click rate using the total number of people who have opened your email.

When I did my test, the norm was to calculate click rate by using the total number of emails sent. Today, SendLane and other top autoresponders calculate click rate using the total number of emails opened.

So in our example above, if 10,000 emails are sent and 200 people click the link, you have a 2% click through rate.

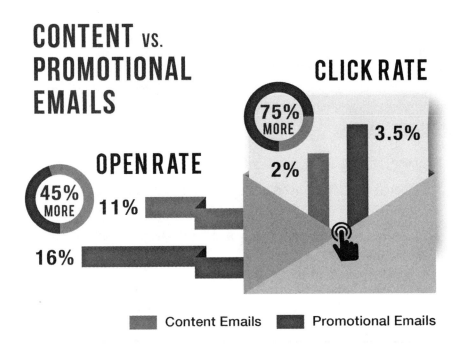

The moral of this story?

Don't be afraid to promote a product to your subscribers. And don't be afraid to make some money!

CHAPTER 9: MONETIZING YOUR AUDIENCE

STARTING TO MAKE MONEY

If you focus on…

1. Delivering value to your email list

2. Using a mix of the three email types described in the previous chapter, and

3. Promoting and endorsing good products for your subscribers to buy, then you're in the perfect position to start monetizing your list.

After all, as we discovered in our case studies, once your subscribers trust you and become your raving fans, they actually want you to recommend products to them.

The steps in this book are specifically designed to help you start generating positive income very quickly. The best part is that the actual business can be launched fairly fast.

Unlike any other business model in the world - online or offline - when you use the Circle of Profit,

- You never have to wait months or invest thousands of dollars to start seeing money coming in.
- You never have to knock down the doors of banks hoping for a loan.
- You don't have to negotiate with a venture capitalist to raise startup money.
- Your new startup can be profitable in a matter of days.

Not only do you start generating profit quickly using the Circle of Profit, but you are immersed in your own personal passion. There is truly no business model in this world that offers you this kind of freedom.

When you finish building your own complete Circle of Profit, you will have all the tools and knowledge that you need to turn your passion into $1 million. You will need to follow every step of this proven process, however.

You may have some hard days ahead, and I guarantee you'll encounter obstacles. But you absolutely can and will turn your passion into $1 million. It might not happen overnight. But it definitely won't happen without implementing every step as detailed in the Circle of Profit.

THE TWO QUICKEST WAYS TO GENERATE PROFITS FROM DAY ONE

As we discussed earlier, the most profitable way to monetize your email list is to create and promote your own passion product. Doing this will probably take a few weeks - maybe even a few months.

So, instead of letting all this time go by without creating income, Phase 1 will help you start generating income immediately.

During Phase 1, you will simply promote products that have been created by others in your niche. When you do this, you are referred to as an "affiliate" for the product that you are promoting.

When you promote products as an affiliate, you can start making money very quickly using these two strategies:

1. The Thank You Page (TYP): Generate sales the instant a new subscriber joins your list.

2. Broadcast Messages promoting other products: Send an email to your list endorsing another product, and get paid in commission on those sales.

QUICK PROFIT STRATEGY 1: THE TYP METHOD

What if I told you that you could immediately start generating money from your list the very second that someone subscribed to your newsletter? That means that the instant someone gives you their email address, you can start to create a profit. I call this the Thank You Page Method, or TYP Method. This method alone has changed the lives of countless students of mine.

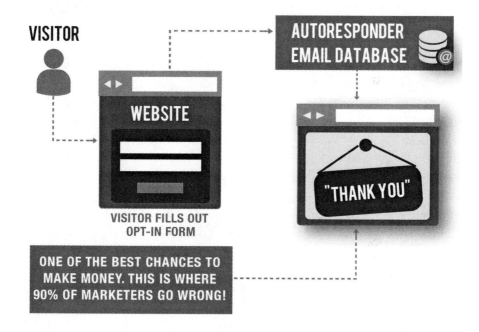

When someone enters an email address on your opt-in page, two things happen:

1. The email is sent to an autoresponder and stored in a database.
2. The person is redirected to a "Thank You" page.

It's called a Thank You Page because the page typically thanks the person for subscribing. About 90% of Thank You Pages are a boring white page with a generic thank you message. Every time I see this, it breaks my heart because I know first-hand that a huge profit opportunity is being missed.

Redirecting new subscribers to a blank Thank You page is a big mistake that is made all the time on the Internet. Why? Because the best time to sell something is when you have your prospect's interest and attention!

Consider these common scenarios:

- A woman is checking her email. She sees a small advertisement and passively clicks it to see what it is about.
- A man lands on your website, likes your free offer and decides to enter his email address. He's eager to get the information promised, so as soon as he puts his email address in, he's interested to see what is on the next page.

You will have a much easier time selling the person in scenario B. He is already paying attention to you. He has already said YES to your offer and shown that he trusts you. This new subscriber is fully engaged at this moment.

But so many marketers still don't know that they can control the look and feel of their TYP, and they leave it like this boring standard one:

The Thank You page is the most chronically wasted real estate on the Internet. And there's no excuse for one, because even the simplest autoresponders allow you to copy and paste any link you want into the thank you field!

You do not have to keep the standard boring thank you page. Instead, you can and should direct your new subscriber to the page of your choice. In fact, even if you simply copy and paste an affiliate link into your thank you field, you will make much more money than using the typical standard page.

There are two ways to deploy the TYP Method:

1. Forward the new subscriber directly to an affiliate offer (someone else's product sales message), or
2. Forward the new subscriber to your own offer.

Assuming that we are still in Phase 1, we are going to use the first TYP strategy above and forward your subscribers to affiliate offers. It's very simple.

Here's how:

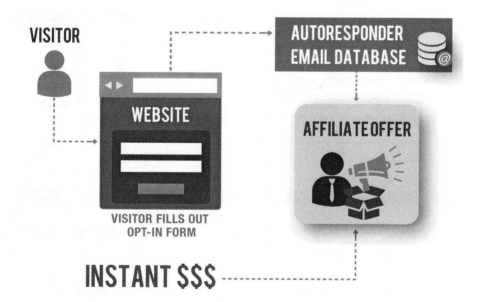

Find your affiliate link for a good product with a strong marketing message. I will use Clickbank.com as an example. Clickbank is a marketplace for online educational products that you can instantly promote and earn up to 75% commission. This is an excellent company that always pays on time and is trustworthy.

Go to Clickbank and get your own link. It takes about 30 seconds. This link allows Clickbank to track every visitor you send to the website. If anyone buys from them after having clicked your link, you automatically earn a commission (a percentage of the total sale – as high as 75%).

There are many other companies like Clickbank. The term affiliate link is common to all of them. Here's an example of a Clickbank.com affiliate link:

Simply copy your link and paste it into the Thank You URL field in your autoresponder. That's it.

Now, when anyone subscribes to your list, they will be directed to the affiliate offer, which is tracked to you. Some of your new subscribers will choose to make a purchase right away. When they do, you make a commission!

QUICK PROFIT STRATEGY 2: AFFILIATE MARKETING THROUGH BROADCASTING

As I mentioned in the previous chapter, it's important that you send out promotional emails. Your list is more active when you actually send product endorsements, so it's a win-win for you.

Even though I like to spend the first 10 days helping the subscriber get to know me using pre-logged autoresponder messages, my most active broadcasting starts on Day 11. I want to note, however, that I also promote and endorse products during those first 10 days. Even when I am building a relationship with my list using pre-logged messages, I still participate in product endorsements.

But my most active affiliate promotions begin on Day 11 using broadcasts.

INSIDE THE CIRCLE: VIDEO BREAK #7

How I Communicate With My Subscribers For The First 10 Days
Find Out More In This Free Video:
www.lurn.com/blog/first10days

First, I find a good product that I believe can help my subscribers. I also make sure that this product has a strong sales message aimed at getting a high sales conversion rate

Next, I follow a simple email template to write two to three emails endorsing the product. Then, I log into SendLane and schedule these broadcast emails to go out over a period of three to four days.

Remember, I like to send my list an email every day, but I don't promote a product every day. I usually follow a schedule like this one.

One Week Email Broadcasting Schedule

Monday: General Content Email to prepare your subscribers for your
                promotions
Tuesday: Promotional Email 1
Wednesday: Promotional Email 2
Thursday: Break
Friday: Promotional Email 3
Saturday: Content or Relationship-Building Email
Sunday: Break

This is just an example and can be altered as you wish, but no matter what, always keep the word "value" in your mind. Even when you're promoting affiliate offers or using the TYP Method, you should only be endorsing products that you believe in and that you know will provide value for your subscriber.

Beware: The easiest way to kill your email list and destroy your subscriber relationships is by endorsing a bad product solely for the purpose of making the most money. Trust me. Your subscribers will disappear if they don't trust you.

So here we are:

- You now have an opt-in page ready to go.
- You have your TYP Method in place so you can make money right away.
- You're ready to communicate with your list as soon as you start getting subscribers.
- Now it's time to go out and find subscribers by getting people to visit your new opt-in page.

CHAPTER 10: ATTRACTING YOUR AUDIENCE

In the last few chapters, you have learned how Phase 1 works. You now know what an opt-in page is. You are ready to start making money by promoting other people's products. You have almost everything you need, but you are missing one critical piece:

You need to get people to your opt-in page so they can give you their email address.

The truth is that you can have the most jaw dropping opt-in page in the world, but if nobody is visiting that page, you'll never make a penny. This is where the concept of traffic comes in.

Traffic refers to the people who are visiting your website.

As I've mentioned before, one of the many miracles of the Internet is that getting traffic is remarkably easy and inexpensive. With a tiny budget, your page can start getting traffic within minutes from major search engines and websites like Google, Facebook, Bing, and more.

Getting traffic to your website is now efficient, cost-effective, and systematic. You can get traffic with even the smallest shoestring budget, and in many cases, you can even get traffic to your opt-in page for free. I'll introduce you to both worlds; you can choose from there.

If you want targeted traffic fast, you will need a tiny budget to invest in getting that traffic. We call this investment traffic.

However, if you want only free traffic, then you will need to invest time in order to get it. This is the traffic trade-off when you're just getting started: money versus time.

If you have a little money to invest in your new business, you can get quick results by investing even just a few hundred dollars. The great news is that if you use the TYP Method, you will typically get a large portion of that investment back immediately, and the rest is usually back in your pocket within the first 30 days.

If you don't want to invest any money, then be prepared to spend some time to develop content to fuel your traffic acquisition. It takes time to create content and time to let that content syndicate over the Internet.

There are many ways to get traffic to your opt-in page. Take a look at just some of your options:

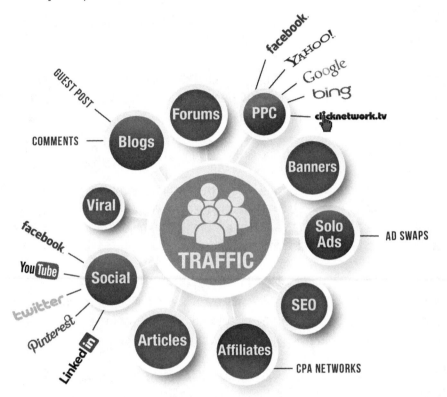

As you can see, there are many options for getting traffic. The sheer volume of choices can be both confusing and intimidating. To help, I've narrowed down your choices to the few that I find to be the most efficient and safe for people who are just starting out.

These are the three sources of traffic that you should focus on for now. The first two require a small investment, and the third is free.

FAST TRAFFIC OPTION #1: EMAIL MEDIA

Email media is by far the best source of investment traffic for starting your email list. This traffic is fast, highly targeted, and virtually guaranteed to work. Email media works in a similar way to buying an advertising slot on a TV station or a radio station. However, instead of buying a 30 second commercial, you are buying a dedicated email drop.

Let me explain:
Bob has an email list of 100,000 subscribers who are all interested in personal development. Bob sends out daily emails with great content and occasional promotions.

Many people in Bob's position offer email advertising to their list. The most common way to do this is using a solo ad. When you buy a solo ad from Bob, you write an email promoting yourself and your product, and he sends that email to his list. Bob has the right to approve it, but the only content in that email is written by you.

In your email, you include a link that Bob's subscribers can click. In the Circle of Profit model, that link goes straight to your opt-in page.

Now subscribers from Bob's email list start to join your email list.

Bob can charge you for your solo ad one of two different ways:

1. A set price, or flat fee, to send out the email, or
2. A fee per number clicks generated by the email.

INSIDE THE CIRCLE: VIDEO BREAK #8

How Email Media Works
Learn All About It Here In This Free Video:
www.lurn.com/blog/emailmedia

FAST TRAFFIC OPTION #2: FACEBOOK ADS

Over a billion people use Facebook to connect with their friends, favorite brands, and more. That's why Facebook is one of the major platforms to utilize in your business.

I use Facebook daily in my own business. The platform has been one of my major customer acquisition strategies for the past two years. I used Facebook advertising to build a 10,000+ subscriber list in only a few months with a very small investment and the Circle of Profit system.

I also used Facebook to create a community of 33,000+ highly engaged members in my own niche. Within three months, I had recovered all of my Facebook advertising expenses, and now I am back in the black - or "in the green" if you like!

What's more, I now own a very sizable list and a large community that I can monetize for as long as I want.

Unlike most online advertising that reaches only 38% of its intended audience, Facebook's average reach is 89%. So essentially, with Facebook, your business gets more exposure and more value from every ad.

In my opinion, Facebook is the new Google and if you haven't used it yet, I recommend that you start now. More than anything, if you haven't started using The Circle of Profit, you better start using that now, too!

Zane Baker
Lurn Student and
Successful Internet Marketer

There are a few things I absolutely love about getting traffic from Facebook:
1. No matter what niche you're in, Facebook has targeted traffic.
2. You can start generating traffic for as little as $20 - often even less.
3. You can get your targeting to be very specific.
4. If done right, the traffic can be very inexpensive.

Facebook now has over 1.23 billion users. If it was a country, it would be the third largest in the world. So no matter what your topic, Facebook has millions of people you can quickly target.

Facebook also has an impeccably easy-to-use advertising system - one of the simplest I have ever seen. Just log in, take 30 seconds to initiate your advertising account, and specify your desired target and budget.

That's it.

Facebook then reviews your ad and your landing page. They have been known to approve ads in as little as 15 minutes or, from what I've seen, a maximum of 12 hours.

Here is the process to expect when you advertise with Facebook:
You give Facebook a few targeting qualifications to zero in on your target customer (such as age range, geographic location, and interests). They show your ad only to those targeted people.

Let's call your ideal target visitor "Sally."

Sally logs in to Facebook to see what's happening in her social world. As she scrolls through her newsfeed, she starts seeing small ads on her screen as well.

Your ad suddenly catches her eye. Sally finds the promise in your ad and clicks it. Now Sally has landed on your opt-in page.

Advertising with Facebook isn't quite as straightforward as email media solo ads. But it is a powerful and scalable traffic generator, and I recommend that you consider adding Facebook to your traffic acquisition strategy as soon as you can.

SALLY'S FB ACCOUNT

YOUR OPT-IN PAGE

YOUR EMAIL LIST

SALLY CLICKS YOUR AD

FREE OFFER FOR EMAIL ADDRESS

FACEBOOK USER ENTERS EMAIL

NOW YOUR SUBSCRIBERS

INSIDE THE CIRCLE: VIDEO BREAK #9

How Facebook Advertising Works
Learn More! Just Go To The Link Below:
www.lurn.com/blog/facebook

FAST TRAFFIC OPTION #3: FORUM COMMENTING

If you are looking for a 100% free source of traffic, your best bet is to find a forum related to your topic and become a contributor.

It's pretty straightforward: Contribute to whatever discussion is going on, and gently promote your opt-in page at the same time. Be careful not to promote your opt-in page in your actual posts; that level of promotion is rarely allowed in most forum communities.

In most forums all you need to have is a static signature file below every post you enter. Believe it or not, these signatures are read pretty closely. I remember doing a test once and finding that with a strongly written signature file, I was able to get close to 20% of those who opened the discussion thread to click my link.

Many of the big forums can easily generate 2,000+ views on a good topic you post. If you can grab 20% of that 2,000, you will get over 400 free views per topic that you start on the forum. Imagine if you start two new topics per day. That's a potential 800+ visitors to your website daily and for free - simply from participating in an online community.

When using forums, always remember to focus on providing value to the other members - and never come across as a spammer.

How forum marketing works:

Let's say a guy named Dave is cruising around a wristwatch forum. He's a big fan of watches. He has a tendency to participate in a lot of watch discussions. He checks the forum at least once a day to stay current on the latest, hottest watch topics.

He sees a topic that interests him and he opens it to start reading and learning more. The first post he sees is by you. You've written a detailed post explaining something. Dave is hooked by your content so he reads it all the way through. As he finishes your post, he sees your signature file at the bottom:

The signature shows your name, your website address, and a catchy phrase like "Learn How To Get Designer Watches For 50% Off – Free Report!"

Dave is intrigued and clicks the link. He lands at your opt-in page and decides to share his email address with you to get his free report. This is precisely how we get free traffic using forums.

It's a very powerful traffic strategy. Actually, forum marketing is how I made my first $10,000 on the Internet. Let's dive more into that right now.

INSIDE THE CIRCLE: VIDEO BREAK #10

How To Get Free Traffic From Forums
Go Here To Watch This Free Video:
www.lurn.com/blog/forumtraffic

THE TRUTH BEHIND MY FIRST $10,000 ONLINE

Remember in Chapter 1 how I started out, struggling for 18 months, trying to make money online? That was 2002, and I was just 19 years old. I was so addicted to learning how to make money online that I started skipping classes. Sometimes I even went days without any sleep.

I had one dream: Make $10,000 per month on my own. I was tortured by the thought of "doing what everyone does." I couldn't bear the idea of ending up in a normal, boring job. So I set out on a road of my own.

I wanted to control my own destiny, but the road was not easy. Many times, I felt like quitting. I was plagued by a nagging feeling that getting a job would be easier and less stressful. But I refused to give up. I could feel the dream. I felt like I could see it; it was near!

For 18 months I banged my head against the wall looking for the secret key to online success. I bought products. I bought software. I went to workshops. I went to seminars. I hired coaches. I did it all. But after 18 months, I still had not made a dime.

And then, on the advice of a forum member, I learned the secret. This was it. I decided that this was the day my life would change forever. "If this doesn't work," I said to myself, "I'm getting a J.O.B."

I worked for 24 hours straight, and woke up to $300 in my bank account. I had finally cracked the code.

And in the next 60 days I earned over $10,000.

So why am I telling you this story again? Because I made all that first money online using free traffic from forums!

Forums are an excellent source of free traffic, but you need to put in a lot of time to get significant results. You need to commit to spending at least 30 minutes a day commenting on forums in your niche. If you are consistent, you should see a steady stream of traffic coming to your opt-in page.

These three sources of traffic are a great start, but they're only the tip of the iceberg. There are many, many other options.

CHAPTER 11: BECOME A TRUE AUTHORITY

You now have everything you need to start building your own list of raving fans and to start making money. You know how to create a killer opt-in page that converts. You know how to get as much opt-in page traffic as your heart desires, to build your email list. You also know how to communicate with your subscribers in a way that builds trust.

If you really want to see success fast, stop thinking about money and start thinking about subscribers. No matter what niches I enter, I consistently find that each subscriber on my mailing list is worth anywhere between $.50 to $3 per month in revenue.

In other words, if I have a list of 10,000 subscribers, and I manage it properly, I should be able to generate at least $5,000 to $30,000 a month.

It's a beautifully simple profit formula: The more subscribers you add, the more money you make. It becomes a wonderful circle of profit: New subscribers lead to more profit, which earns you more money (to invest in more traffic if you want) to acquire new subscribers, which lead to even more profit.

Branding

While you are using the Circle of Profit to start and grow your business, there's an important word you should keep in mind as we go into Phase 2: Branding.

Branding is one of those terms you hear all the time, but you rarely hear why it is important. Here's why: Creating a strong brand means that your target market feels that you are a trusted and reliable source of what they seek.

We talked a lot about relationship-building during Phase 1. Creating that strong relationship is important because it means you are training each of your subscribers to look at you as an authority in your niche topic. Your subscribers need to feel that any time they need help in that niche, you are the best source of information and guidance.

The more the subscriber views you as an authority, the stronger your business becomes - and the more profit you will generate. And when you get into developing your own information product, this niche authority branding will prove to be even more critical to your success.

As you build your business, it is imperative that you remain consistently mindful of your brand. Pay special attention to the products you promote, the messages you send, and how you portray yourself.

I always recommend taking a moment before sending out any email. Ask yourself, "Is this strengthening my brand, or is it weakening it?" Sometimes I have to reject promoting a certain product - even if it's a great one - because I believe that endorsing it will negatively impact my brand.

When endorsing other people's products, I always review the sales material first. I always review the content of the product, and I always do my background research on the person who is teaching the course. I have to take responsibility for what I am sending to my subscribers because they trust me. If there is even one small thing about the product that could hurt my brand, I won't promote the product.

Beyond the types of emails you send, there are wonderful tools out there to make it even easier to create and strengthen your brand as an authority to your subscribers.

As you get ready to build out Phase 2 of your business, you will want to look into having a few types of properties online to help you boost your brand and get your message out.

1. Your own blog
2. Your own YouTube channel. Videos are a powerful way to build relationships and brands.
3. A Facebook page
4. A Twitter account

You do not need to use every one of these, but the more you use, the better your results will be.

I have my own blog, an active YouTube channel, and also a very active Facebook page with nearly 100,000 followers. To this day I have never become interested in Twitter. (That may change.)

When it comes to building your own brand, you have full decision-making authority on what you want to do and which tools you want to use. I am just here to share my experience and give you some ideas.

This is where Phase 1 connects with Phase 2. If you have done your work in Phase 1 and built a strong list with which you have a strong relationship, you are ready to move into Phase 2.

In Phase 2, we plunge into the first major step of turning your passion into $1 million. It's time to really build your business and see that 500% increase in your profits.

Excited? Turn the page and keep going!

SECTION 3: GENERATING $1 MILLION & BECOMING AN AUTHORITY

CHAPTER 12: THE HIDDEN KEY - DIGITAL PRODUCTS

One of my favorite things about the Circle of Profit is its flexibility: You can start with Phase 1 (affiliate marketing), easing your way into Phase 2 (product creation). Or you can jump right into Phase 2, which you're going to learn about now.

This is where it becomes pretty simple to start making six or seven figures. I do it over and over in my business.

You might recognize some of the stories and concepts that you're about to read, like how to choose the right niche. That's because these are key strategies, which you will use whether you're focusing on affiliate marketing or you're moving into the product creation realm.

My goal throughout this book is to explain both phases to you in as much detail as possible. Right now, however, we're zeroing in on Phase 2 of the Circle of Profit: Creating your own digital product.

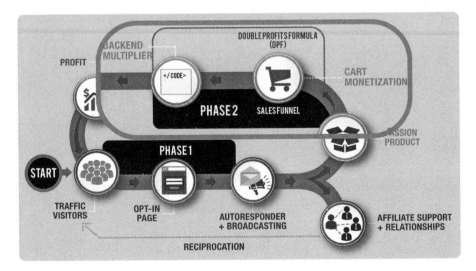

Our Goal: To position you to turn your passion into $1 million. The knowledge you're going to gain now lays the same groundwork that created my $10 million a year business.

Key Concept: The world of information products makes it 100% possible for you to build a business at any scale you desire. I am not the only person who has used information products to create millions of dollars online. Hundreds of others have done the same.

How it works: Phase 1 built your email list full of subscribers who trust you. Now you can monetize those relationships by promoting other people's products as an affiliate and collecting a commission on every sale you refer. This is a fast way to start your business, and the major benefit of affiliate marketing.

But there is a small disadvantage as well.

As an affiliate, you can earn only when you actively promote a product - and there's a limit to the amount you can earn. Your earnings are limited to a maximum of 50% or 75% commission per sale.

"What's wrong with 50% to 75%?" you might wonder. You're right. Those are pretty high commissions.

But think beyond that - like the product owners have.

Product owners are willing to give affiliates like you high commissions because they know they're going to generate much more money from these customers in the long term - by selling them other products directly.

As an affiliate, you don't get any of those future profits; you don't gain any of that "lifetime value."

So, while Phase 1 is an outstanding way for you to start making money fast, you are going to need to become a product owner if you want to build a big business. As a product owner, other affiliates not only promote your products, but they hand you customers who are primed and ready to buy even more from you - directly and forever.

INSIDE THE CIRCLE: VIDEO BREAK #11

What Are Information Products
Learn More! Just Go To The Link Below:
www.lurn.com/blog/informationproducts

THE POWER OF INFORMATION PRODUCTS

Creating and launching your own information product allows you to add unlimited scale to your business.

Here are a few of the enormous benefits of creating your own product:

1. You immediately begin to make 100% rather than only 50% or 75%.
2. You get other affiliates to promote your product and build scale into your business.
3. You can build a strong "back-end" to make far more profits in the lifetime of each customer (you'll learn more about this later in this book).
4. You can build a true asset that has a value in the market. Your product and the business behind it can be sold one day down the line.

With your own product, you get full control over your future. Some students are frightened at the prospect of creating their own information products; they feel incapable - or they don't think they have enough knowledge on the given subject.

If you're one of these apprehensive people, let me tell you very sincerely: You can do it. How? Because a major part of the product-making process can be outsourced. And if you want, you can outsource the entire process!

The Phase 2 formula you are about to learn can empower absolutely anyone in the world to create an internationally best-selling information product. And the best part? You can use it over and over.

When you have your own information products, creating profit comes down to two major factors:

1. Traffic - The people visiting your website (covered previously).
2. Conversion - Your website visitors who become customers (new concept).

Conversion is incredibly important to your success, yet a remarkably simple process. There are really simple formulas you can use to create conversions.

Most new business owners typically struggle to get traffic to their website. Even though we discussed traffic acquisition earlier, it is important to note that in Phase 2, having your own information product can actually open up an entire new world of traffic opportunities.

That's because in Phase 2, you can now bring in people who sell your products for you (affiliates). You do not have to buy the traffic that affiliates generate; you never even have to put up a dime. With affiliate marketing, you only pay when someone makes a sale for you.

PHASE 1: CREATING INITIAL PROFIT
Creating Traffic Using Only Your Own Resources

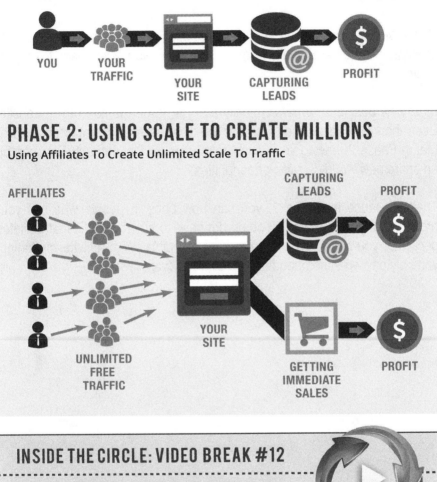

PHASE 2: USING SCALE TO CREATE MILLIONS
Using Affiliates To Create Unlimited Scale To Traffic

INSIDE THE CIRCLE: VIDEO BREAK #12

How Affiliates Promote Your Product For Free
Go Here To Watch This Free Video:
www.lurn.com/blog/affiliates

When you started out, there was just one of you. But now you can partner with an unlimited number of affiliates without incurring any upfront expenses. With hundreds of affiliates working to sell your products, imagine how your profits will multiply.

That's why the secret to turning your passion into $1 million lies in creating and marketing your own information products.

Information Products

Examples of information products include eBooks, audio recordings, and video courses. They're all digital, so you never have to carry any inventory or manage any physical processes. Best of all? Your expenses remain exactly the same whether you sell 10 copies or 10,000 copies.

The best digital products have a nice mix of several media types. An educational course might have some written parts plus video to augment the written portions.

The more kinds of media you provide, the easier it is for your students to consume the content, and the more valuable your product becomes. Everyone is different. Some people like watching a video, and others prefer to read. Providing different kinds of products broadens your product's appeal.

For example, one of my team members and I recently took the same course. I went through the entire course by reading only the PDF summaries of each video. I found this to be much quicker and far more satisfying for my goals.

My colleague, on the other hand, never read a single PDF; she preferred to watch each video. We both got the same end results but we were able to each use our own preferred learning approach.

Creating Information Products

Twenty years ago, creating a product with audio and video was expensive and time consuming. You needed expensive equipment if you wanted to create even a semi-professional product. Video cameras cost nearly $5,000 - and a good microphone could be as expensive as $1,000. That was just the beginning. You also had to hire an entire editing crew to put it all together.

With digital imaging, however, information products are suddenly incredibly easy to create - and on a shoestring budget, too. Most laptops and computers come pre-loaded with the software and hardware needed to do it all yourself.

Even if you need to buy equipment, you can create professional-level content with less than $100 in equipment costs. At this point, though, you don't even need to invest $100. You can create much of your content absolutely free.

HOW I CREATED $1 MILLION FROM MY WIFE'S CLOSET

It's crazy to see how far we've come in technology in the last ten years alone. When I started, if I wanted to get an audio recording done, I had two choices. On the low end, I could spend $5,000 to buy the audio equipment. Or I could choose to spend even more hiring an audio studio.

It was difficult, and it was expensive.

Today, even the least expensive laptop comes with built-in professional grade audio software, and a $100 microphone from your local electronics store will rival that of any professional studio.

In July 2013, I had an idea for a great audio product that I wanted to create in the personal development niche. However, it was important to me that the product be of high quality.

I began exploring how to get my product created. You won't believe what I figured out.

I discovered the best audio studio in the world - and it cost absolutely nothing: My wife's closet.

You see, my wife's closet is full of clothes. There is no better way to dampen an echo than to surround yourself with clothes! I dragged a chair into the closet. There was an ironing board in there already, so I set my laptop on the board and held my microphone right in my hand.

In less than five hours (all in just one day), I recorded an amazing, professional-grade dream product that would impact the lives of thousands of people.

I went on to create over $1 million in sales in less than a year with that audio product. My only expense? The microphone, which is mine forever to use for as many products as I want.

Who would have thought that the more clothes my wife buys, the more money I can make!

INSIDE THE CIRCLE: VIDEO BREAK #13

**What Equipment You Need To Create
An Information Product**
Find Out Now! Watch This Free Video:
www.lurn.com/blog/equipment

Seriously. The key is to provide valuable content. And today, accessing the tools to produce that content is the easiest part. If you've got valuable content, you can have your digital information product done in just one day if you want. Take the time to create excellent content so that you can attract hordes of raving fans all over the world.

Next, I'm going to show you how to create information products worth $1 million. I will also share my secrets to help you multiply your profits from each of your customers.

CHAPTER 13: THE 3 PARTS TO CREATING A $1 MILLION INFORMATION PRODUCT

Now I'm going to take you through a crash course on how to simply and quickly create your first profitable information product. There are three main steps that you will follow.

Each step is broken down into small, actionable steps.

Step #1 sets you up to choose the right topic, right from the beginning. I will give you the details of the crucial 5 metric topic checklist. Going through this process virtually guarantees that you have chosen a niche that can generate $1 million or more.

In Step #2, you are going to learn how to create your own information product. I will show you a process that makes it possible for you to get as much help as you need from outside sources.

Finally, in Step #3, we will discuss your sales process creation. You will be able to use automated tools to create your own members' area and even back-end monetization. Our focus here will be to create the highest lifetime value possible for every single one of your new customers.

JON'S STORY

He was a student full of talent, life, and an amazing message to share with the world. By the time he came to me, Jon Talarico was already a huge success in his business and life. However, it wasn't always this way. Jon had quite a life and had to fight his way to get to where he is today...

Just a few years before I met Jon, he was broke, in-debt, and even homeless. He grew up in a small town in Michigan with little to no opportunity. He ventured out into the world to find his calling, but he learned how difficult it can be to truly find it.

Jon, more than anyone else I've ever met, has an incredible fighting spirit. He discovered he had an amazing skill at building relationships. Jon can sit down with a complete stranger and know their entire life story in about six minutes flat. I have personally seen him build relationships with kings, celebrities, and top athletes all over the world.

This became his saving grace. Jon used his networking ability to open up opportunity after opportunity. He went from being homeless to owning a professional sports franchise, having an office in the Empire State Building, and flying around the world in private jets meeting celebrities and politicians.

As you can see, Jon has great wisdom and knowledge to share. He has turned his experience, knowledge, and talent into a system. Before he knew it, he was coaching his friends and family into becoming great successes as well.

Given he could only work with people one on one, his ability to take his education to the world was limited. What he really needed to do was create an online course. Deep down Jon knew this was the solution to changing more lives; however, he was scared. This fear stopped him from making progress for years.

Jon had one big question that plagued him: "How do I build an online course? How do I put value into something that students will want to actually buy from me? I've never created a course or been a teacher..."

This was when Jon turned to me. He wanted to know if I could guide him through the process.

I gave Jon a simple piece of advice: break it down into manageable pieces, and don't worry about being perfect.

It was not easy. Like many students, Jon would continue to get stuck by thinking about the future steps involved. He focused on all the things he did not know. This lead to more fear which again slowed him down. I have seen this happen with many students and clients.

However, my next piece of advice seemed to make a breakthrough: "Just create your product outline. That's it. Don't think of anything else right now."

I have taught every client I've worked with the same thing: the first step is always to simply structure the program. The more detailed of an outline you can create, the easier it will be for you to launch your entire information business.

Immediately, Jon advanced in his product creation process. He went from doubting whether he could ever build his own digital product to now owning one of the Industry's top rated "opportunity" courses. He is traveling the world and reaching thousands of students.

All of this great success has come simply because one evening Jon sat down and created an outline: he scribbled down 4 module titles. Then, under each module he added about six to nine bullet points (these are called sections).

To make the content filming process easy, he added four more bullet points under each section to give them structure.

That's it.

Believe it or not, doing this simple "bullet point" exercise made Jon create his entire online course in a matter of just days.

Jon admits that you should focus all your early efforts on simple steps. Don't let yourself get intimated and bogged down by the big picture. Instead, start by creating an outline and move onto the next small step!

CHAPTER 14: STEP #1
IS IT A $1 MILLION NICHE?

When I first started trying to make money online, I made a crucial mistake that cost me seven months - and the little money I had.

I mentioned in Chapter 4 that I choose the wrong passion niche in which to launch my business. I jumped the gun without doing my research and I made the incorrect assumption that my idea would be incredibly profitable.

That was the first (and last) time I ever made that mistake. Here's the full story of what happened:

The #1 Lesson I Learned Through Failure

When I first started learning about online marketing, I was fortunate that I found a forum. Back then we didn't have any training like this book or online step-by-step systems.

I had to really piece it together myself.

I made the best I could of this forum. Sometimes I would spend hours on it studying what people were doing; asking questions and clicking every link I could.

After months and months of research, I arrived at a simple evaluation: Everyone on this forum seemed so "normal." They were just everyday people who were having amazing success online. I had found exactly what I was searching for.

But there was one major problem.

Although the people on this forum were very helpful, no one seemed to really have a "system." Running an online information marketing business was so new that everyone succeeding had done it through countless hours of work, dead ends, and pure brute force.

They had each tried many different tactics until one happened to work. Many times, even they weren't sure what they had done that had led to their own success.

I spent a lot of time on this forum and eventually I grew impatient. I wanted to start my business. But since I had to accept that there was no existing system, I had to take my best shot.

I made a very simple evaluation: "People are taking a topic that they love or that they are good at, creating an information product, throwing it up on the Internet, and making tons of money!" Back in Chapter 4, I mentioned that I was very good at little hacks and tricks to getting good grades and acing exams. Naturally, I thought "How to Easily Ace Exams!" was my perfect niche topic!

You'll recall I was thrilled to discover that there was not a single competitor in the market. I thought "I'm going to be an instant millionaire!" What I did not know was that this lack of competition was what should have steered me away from that niche.

But I soldiered on, building my product for seven months and spending every penny I had. Nothing happened. Not even one sale. My seven months of hard work had been for nothing. I had failed.

Today, I firmly believe in researching any idea I have. I don't believe in taking big risks - only very well-calculated ones.

Although most passions can be turned into $1 million, there are certain passions that cannot. So how do you know what's going to work and what won't?

In this chapter, I've distilled my knowledge and experience in topic selection to five simple points on a checklist. These are the topic-qualifying metrics that you absolutely must measure before ever launching in a niche.

With this 5-step checklist and less than 60 minutes, you can determine which of your passions will be the most profitable.

The 5 steps to qualifying your passion topic:

1. Information Friendly
2. Competition
3. Size of Audience
4. Popularity in Search
5. Long-Term Potential

Checking off some of these steps takes only seconds. Others may take a bit more time to research, but you'll also learn how to find and use some great free online tools that automatically do the work for you.

RESEARCH METRIC #1: IS THE PRODUCT INFORMATION FRIENDLY?

Remember the underwear example I used a few chapters back? There are literally billions of people who wear underwear around the world. There is an incredible demand for underwear, too. We can even find lots of people looking for underwear online.

But if you wanted to create an information product about underwear, could you? No. I use this extreme example to make a point. You need to think through and understand the concept behind it. Many times we have a hobby or a passion that is simply not information-friendly.

There are no real tools to be used for this step; it is mostly your thought process. However, if you can't figure out whether your passion is information friendly or not, move to Step #2 - it will take care of that for you.

RESEARCH METRIC #2: IS THERE COMPETITION?

Finding competition is excellent news for your niche. It means that other people are already having success, and you can too. If, however, you find that your niche has no competition, stay away. It's very likely that no one's selling it because it doesn't sell.

To find out whether there are others already selling products similar to yours online, there are three excellent sources of competition data:

1. Clickbank.com
2. Udemy.com
3. Google.com

95% of the time, Clickbank and Udemy will give you enough of an idea to know whether to proceed. Clickbank is the #1 marketplace for digital information products, and Udemy is fast on the rise as #2. Between these two platforms, over 30,000 online courses are offered.

They have covered every niche that you can imagine. If you cannot find a similar course to your idea in these 30,000 courses, your idea is far too risky. You need to pick a different topic.

Do not try to bypass this rule. The odds are massively stacked against you if you do. It is especially important when you are just starting out that you stick to proven niches.

So let me say this once more: If you do not find competition, stop your research immediately, change topics and start at #1 again. Your topic must pass all five points on this checklist. No exceptions.

INSIDE THE CIRCLE: VIDEO BREAK #14

Finding Products In Your Niche To Verify Your Idea
Get Started! Free Video Below:
www.lurn.com/blog/productidea

RESEARCH METRIC #3: WHAT IS THE SIZE OF THE AUDIENCE?

I was once talking on the phone to my friend Fred Lam, the founder of iPro Academy. I was telling him about a student of mine who had a crazy niche idea: Teaching people about ice fishing.

I hadn't heard much about this topic and wasn't sure if it was going to be a viable niche.

I mentioned it to Fred in passing, expressing that I was concerned and did not know how many people in the world cared about ice fishing. What he said next shocked me.

"That's easy, Anik. Give me a minute. OK… So for ice fishing, there are about 1,196,820 million people in the United States alone who are active...84% of them are men, so your marketing should focus on men."

I cannot tell you how far my jaw fell to the ground. I thought he was joking. I thought he had made it all up just to poke fun at me. When I realized he hadn't been joking and asked him to explain himself, he started laughing and showed me just how he had calculated this data.

He was using the free tool I mentioned briefly back in Chapter 4: Facebook's Audience Insights, which lets you dissect a niche and figure out the right target for yourself.

Facebook's Audience Insights doesn't cost a penny. You don't even have to have any ads running on Facebook to use it. In fact, it is specifically made to be a planning tool, and it is my favorite tool now.

If I type in "ice fishing" and focus on the U.S., here's what I get:

If you have a Facebook account, simply go to ads.facebook.com and sign up to be an advertiser. (Even if you have to enter your credit card number, you will not be billed.) Once you are in the advertising area, go to "Tools" and click on "Audience Insights."

It's a fast process and will become one of your favorite audience research tools moving forward.

To keep things simple when I am researching the size of an audience, I only search the following countries, all proven to have active online shoppers.

1. United States
2. Canada
3. United Kingdom
4. Australia
5. New Zealand

You can add other countries as well. However, these five countries will give you a great idea of your audience size.

How big should your audience be? Nothing is written in stone, but here are some average numbers to use as a general idea.

Size of Audience	Rating
Less than 200,000	Not recommended.
200,001 – 500,000	Good niche. Has limits, but can work.
500,001 – 1,000,000	Good niche. Can reach $1 million mark.
1,000,001 – 3,000,000	Great niche. Lots of potential.
3,000,001 – 7,000,000	Huge potential. I recommend choosing a sub-niche to enter niche.
7,000,001+	Choose a sub-niche! This one is too broad.

Again, these numbers are not written in stone. Each case is different. These are simply to give you a rough idea on where to get started.

INSIDE THE CIRCLE: VIDEO BREAK #15

How To Analyze The Size Of Your Market
Go Here To Watch This Free Video:
www.lurn.com/blog/marketsize

RESEARCH METRIC #4: ARE PEOPLE ACTIVELY SEEKING YOUR INFORMATION?

Using a couple of other great free tools, you can know in just minutes whether there are enough people around the world who share your passion enough to actually research it online.

Keyword research tools let you take a peek behind the search engines of the world, especially Google. You simply type in a keyword to instantly see how many people around the world have searched for that keyword recently. You can also narrow your results to specific countries if you want.

Here are two great tools to find your actively-searching market size:

1. **Google Adwords Keyword Planner**
2. SEMRush.com - Provides 10 free searches

Google Adwords Keyword Planner

Google's Keyword Planner is by far the most popular of these tools. There is a catch, however: To gain access, you need to activate an advertising account by creating a fictitious ad and entering your credit card details. At the last moment, you can turn the ad off and never spend a dime - but you can still gain full access to their free keyword research tool.

SEMRush

The process of having to pretend to launch an ad and also enter a credit card number makes some students feel uncomfortable. This kind of keyword research, at early niche evaluation stage, does not usually require an advanced tool like Google's Keyword Planner.

An alternate option for our students is www.SEMRush.com. It's free, instant, and provides enough information to help you determine the size of your niche.

The following screenshots were taken at the time of the writing of this book. The user interface may be slightly different now, but the service should remain the same.

First, go to www.SEMRush.com.

Next, figure out a good keyword that represents your niche. For example, if you want to build a business around the world of personal development, perhaps your niche is information about the law of attraction. You'll type "law of attraction" into the keyword search area.

Or let's say you are passionate about weight loss and fitness. You could start your search by typing "weight loss" into the keyword area.

Your keyword should be targeted... but also general. "Law of attraction" is a perfect keyword to analyze the niche; "how to apply the law of attraction" is too specific for this purpose.

The next page you get will look something like this:

There are a few things to note here:

1. Data from only the United States is selected.
This is absolutely fine for the purpose of our search. We are simply trying to see the demand of one niche idea versus another one. In this scenario, we do not need to dig any deeper.

2. The search volume is 40,500 times per month, the number of monthly searches for that keyword averaged over a 12-month period.
This does not mean that your market only has 40,500 people in it. There are literally hundreds of different keywords that target your passion. If we total them all up, you will likely see numbers in the hundreds of thousands, if not millions.

It's important to remember that at this point, we are simply doing a quick "lay of the land" search. Our purpose now is strictly to get a strong feeling that there is indeed demand for your niche. In this scenario, we only need to use a few keywords to get that result.

Let's compare this to another niche idea to show you the drastic difference with a slightly less marketable niche - say, your passion for skipping rocks?

Here's what you'll see:

Vast difference, right? "Law of attraction" has 40,500 searches while "rock skipping" has only 320 searches. Now you can start to see what it takes to get a sizable market.

After spending months playing with this tool, I calculated the following rough estimates.

No. Of Searches	Rating
0 – 3,000	Absolutely Not a Profitable Niche
3,001 – 5,000	Slightly Profitable Niche
5,001 – 15,000	$1 Million Niche (Sweet Spot)
15,001 – 40,000	Very Profitable (but competitive)
40,001+	Incredibly Profitable (very competitive)

As always, there are exceptions, and every product is different. These numbers might not be completely accurate for every niche. I simply typed in niches that I know to be excellent and compared the search volumes with niches that I know to be bad.

INSIDE THE CIRCLE: VIDEO BREAK #16

How To Do Keyword Research
Learn How By Watching This Video:
www.lurn.com/blog/keywordresearch

This is just the beginning. The first major step here is to make sure that your passion has at least 5,000 monthly searches on this tool. As far as competition is concerned, I have never worried too much about it. There will always be opportunities in the most competitive niches if you use our system.

One last important note: Just because a niche has 100,000 or more searches does not necessarily make it a great topic for you to pursue as a business. You still have to be sure that all the other checkpoints in this list have been marked off with a big positive "Yes."

The next step guarantees that your niche is profitable as well.

RESEARCH METRIC #5: LONG-TERM SPENDING CAPABILITY

Is your niche an idea that comes and goes? Or will you be able to build a customer for life?

Look at golfing as an example. If you were to join my list today and buy a golfing product, there is a strong chance that you will still be into golfing three years from now - and probably even ten years from now.

Here is another example: I have a student who is very successful in the pregnancy niche. She is a certified pediatric nurse and absolutely loves working with new mothers. Initially, I was worried for her because this niche does not pass the fifth step on the checklist.

Think about it: Pregnancy only lasts nine months. After that, the new mother is no longer seeking information on pregnancy, so she is no longer a customer. However, as I said, this particular student is still very successful because of the sheer size of the demand for her niche.

As she grows, she is starting a new topic in her business: Infant care.

Now her business will progress right alongside her customers. This will significantly increase the value of each customer she brings in.

The higher the long-term capability, the more scalable your business can be. So if your niche does not have long-term scalability, then the size of your short-term demand needs to make up for the lack of long-term potential. Alternately, you can choose related sub-niches to your main niche to grow the topics covered and make your business scalable that way.

There you have it!

These are the only five steps you need to know to choose the right niche. As long as you cross check your digital publishing business ideas along these lines, you will remove 90% of your risk.

TY'S STORY

Before getting into digital publishing, Ty Cohen was a manager at Walgreens. In his spare time, he collected comic books and action figures and sold them on the Internet. Needless to say, he was a busy man!

He was excited by digital publishing because it could potentially open up free time and allow him to spend more time with his family. Excited by the possibilities, he spent all of his free time researching information marketing and different niches he could start his business in.

As someone who had a passion for comics, he understood that there was a market for people interested in buying and collecting comics and believed that he could create a product that would teach people about collecting comic books and action figures.

His research paid off. He used the Internet as a medium to connect with customers and comic lovers all of the world and this helped scale his business. His first business grew so fast that he was able to quit his job at Walgreens and focus entirely on digital publishing.

That was just the beginning of Ty's journey. He has spent over 10 years building a highly successful digital publishing business. At the same time, he enjoys the freedom of being able to spend time with his family.

In one of his most successful businesses, he is earning around $1,000 a day and this is just one of over 2-dozen websites. He was able to grow and scale this business to earning 50k in just one year. He is on track to do over half a million in sales for the year

Since he has learned how to create digital information products and market them on the Internet, Ty has enlisted his whole family. His wife has been highly successful selling digital information products around her passions. Even his 17-year-old daughter has created a digital publishing business of her own!

Ty himself has expanded his business beyond comics and action figures. He's a perfect example of how many options you have when you start your digital publishing business. Ty is currently involved with over 2 dozen niches including crochet, men's sexual health, wedding planning, and home schooling for children- specifically African American children. His wife built her business around makeup while his daughter created a business around natural hairstyles.

How does Ty and his family pick their niches? It's NOT only about what they're passionate about. He utilizes websites like Amazon.com and Google's Keyword Planner Tool to discover niches that other people are already interested in and already buying. Instead of trying to reinvent the wheel, just do what already works.

Ty's winning system for creating and marketing products on the Internet starts with a written product. Those are the easiest for him to create. If it does well, he will create an audio product to add more value to his customers.

As a whole, Ty likes to work on products that are simple, easy, and profitable. Ty creates a variety of products with various price points. His lowest ticket item sold for $7.95 while his highest and most successful sold for between $549 and $997.

With the help of websites like guru.com and upwork.com, Ty can get these simple, easy, and profitable new products produced quickly and inexpensively.

Ty is a smart guy, but he started his business with no special advantages. There is no reason why you cannot replicate his success and create a digital publishing business that grows your income and allows you to spend more time with your family, too!

CHAPTER 15: STEP #2
FINDING A GREAT DOMAIN NAME

Finding a domain name is a key step. Don't rush the process. In many cases, my students spend a little time every day researching domain names while moving on to the next steps.

According to the last published number by TechCrunch, there are over 250 million domain names registered around the world and 50% of those are .com names. Obviously, this means that finding a domain name can be tricky. But don't give up.

Head over to GoDaddy.com or NameCheap.com and start typing in your domain name ideas. Search until you find a great domain name that fits most of the criteria given below.

Personally, I use NameCheap.com for all my domain name registrations. Many of our students have preferred GoDaddy.com in the past. But if you are simply researching domain names, I can recommend some tools that will save you a lot of stress and time:

1. LeanDomainSearch.com
2. BustaName.com
3. DomainsBot.com

Our students live off of these tools; the first two are my favorites.

BustaName.com is a great tool. It lets you take a few different words and combine them into a domain name that is available. I highly recommend this tool if you are willing to have three words in your domain name, which works fine.

DomainsBot is a good tool, but since it focuses more on non-.com domain names, I am not a huge fan.

WHAT TO LOOK FOR IN A GOOD DOMAIN NAME

Here are the domain name rules I follow and recommend to students:

1. Use a .com domain. I prefer .com for building a brand.
2. Short, catchy, and memorable. No more than three words.
3. Easy to type and spell. www.yoursubconscious.com is not a good domain name because many people will misspell it.
4. Use power words. The domain name itself should send a message.

Straightforward. Simple. Easy to remember. And powerful. This is what you are looking for in a good domain name.

You can work on this step while you are working on the next steps. If it takes you some time to find the perfect domain name, don't worry. Some of our best students have taken several days to find a domain name they loved.

SHOULD YOU BUY AN EXISTING "PREMIUM" DOMAIN NAME?

It's pretty common to come upon a domain name that you are researching and find that it is for sale as a premium domain name. The decision to buy or not to buy is really your own. If you absolutely love the domain name and can easily afford to pay for it, then go for it.

I have found that getting a super domain name versus getting a good domain name makes almost no difference in your results and profits. And in the end, profits are all we really care about.

Personally, I have chosen to buy many domain names when I felt it was important. However, I never did this when I was just starting out. At the beginning, I recommend that you buy a less-perfect domain name and use your funds instead to invest in traffic.

But again, the choice is completely yours.

If you decide to keep things simple and save money by finding a domain

146

that is still available, the easiest way to do this is to pick three power words and combine them using www.BustaName.com.

If you're still having trouble, keep searching; there has never been a situation in which I or any of my students have not eventually found a great domain name that we love and that does great justice to our online businesses.

Even if you're still looking for the right domain name, you can still keep moving forward and determine what your unique hook is - and what you should name your product.

CHAPTER 16: STEP #3
DISCOVERING YOUR HOOK: NAMING YOUR PRODUCT

Before you can begin to outline and create your product, it's a good idea to name the product. This process of determining the product's hook - the thing that catches your visitor's attention - will actually help you to create the outline. In fact, discovering the hook is often 90% of the battle.

Here are some great hook examples to get you started:

1. How to Lose 10 Pounds in 10 days.
2. The 1 Wall Street Secret That Made This Guy $5 Million
3. How to Make $10,000 in 30 Days or Less
4. 3 Steps to Ranking on Page One of Google in 7 Days or Less
5. 7 Ways to Find the Job of Your Dreams
6. Master Microsoft Excel in Just 5 Hours

As you can see, all of these hooks have one thing in common: They all deliver a specific promise, often within a defined period. The purpose of a hook is to grab your reader's attention almost instantly. A great hook is almost a promise in and of itself.

The key to a hook is to use a powerful statement that delivers a vision or a promise that many in your niche will find enticing. I prefer to use shorter hooks. I always try to get mine into just one sentence. This can be difficult, but if you massage your message for a little while, you should be able to do it.

I also find that one of the easiest ways to come up with a hook is to spy on your top competitors to see what they're doing. What are their hooks? If they are successfully selling their product, it's safe to assume that their hook is working.

Here's how: Go to Clickbank.com or Udemy.com and make a list of the top five products in your category. From there, write down the hooks of those products. You will start to see a trend that you can use as your starting point. Then angle your own hook right there.

NAMING YOUR PRODUCT

The name of your product is an exercise that merges your domain name with your hook. Sometimes, it can be as simple as combining them.

Let's use my product Publish Academy as an example. The name of this product is really Publish Academy: How to Turn Your Passion into $1 Million. The first part (on the left side of the colon) happens to be my domain name, and the second part (on the right side of the colon) is my hook. It worked out perfectly for me!

If you are using a three-word domain name (as discussed in Step 2), you can often very easily make that domain name into your product name.

Remember, you are just starting. Nothing has to be perfect yet. The key is to execute. Do not get stuck on this step. The beauty of a digital business is that you can change anything at any time. The name of the product can even change in the future if you want it to.

For now, pick something powerful that makes a statement and that you like, and run with it!

Now that you have your niche, your domain name, and your hook, it is time to dig into your main product.

We're going to start by creating your product outline.

CHAPTER 17: STEP #4
YOUR PRODUCT OUTLINE

Creating your product outline is most of the battle. But once you have determined the details of your product, the rest is very easy. You can even outsource most of it if you want.

In this book, we are going to cover just one of the ways that you can create your product outline. Your chosen strategies can change somewhat, depending on the kind of product you are creating, its length, and the niche topic.

However, when writing your outline, I recommend the tasks listed in this formula:

Task 1 – Name your modules (modules are the same as chapters)
Task 2 – Name your sections (the same as sub-chapters)
Task 3 – Create bullet points for each section
Task 4 – Assign media formats to each section

This sequence has helped many Lurn Nation students outline their first product in 60 minutes or less.

I am also going to give you a fantastic resource that you can and should use when creating your outline - one which very few information marketers ever use, even though it's only one click away: Amazon.com

Go to Amazon.com and search for a book related to your topic of choice. Now click on the title of the resulting book, and then find the "Look Inside" image that's at the top right corner of the book image.

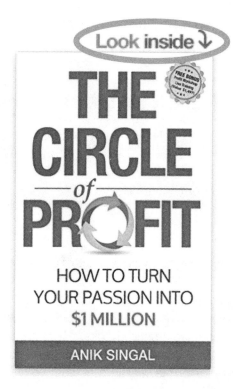

Now click the "Look Inside" image. A new window will open, allowing you to read the first few pages of the book. Amazon usually lets you see at least the table of contents of almost every book it sells.

Can you see where I'm going with this?

I will never, ever condone plagiarizing or copying someone else's hard work. It's not right, and it's not legal.

However, there is absolutely nothing wrong with looking at the top 10 books in your niche and reviewing their tables of contents to determine what topics are the most popular in your niche. I do this all the time, and I suspect most other successful digital marketers do the same.

Scanning the tables of contents of several different books is a great way to spark ideas for your product outlines.

Now that you have this ultimate resource in your hands, let's dive into the details of each task.

TASK 1 – NAME YOUR MODULES (OR CHAPTERS)

When you create a course, call your chapters: modules. The word "module" carries a higher perceived value than the word "chapter." Why? Because most people associate chapters with books, which are usually sold for less than $10. Creating that association in your prospect's mind devalues your course by giving the buyer the feeling that what you're selling is simply a book.

Now break your information product into five to ten modules. That's it.

Task 1 is as simple as that, but don't blow through it without taking the time to research competing products. Always make sure that your product covers the information that your market wants.

TASK 2 – NAME YOUR SECTIONS (OR SUB-CHAPTERS)

Now you're going to break each of your modules down into three to five sections. Again, calling these "sections" increases the perceived value of your course while helping you keep your course organized. Each topic can be easily broken down, assuming that your main module titles are quite general.

This is another task in which looking at tables of contents on Amazon.com can be very helpful.

Here's an example of what you're creating:

Module 1: Introduction and My Story

1. What Is This Book About?
2. Why Am I Writing This Book?
3. What Will You Learn in This Book
4. My Personal Story

Module 2: Determining Your Perfect Weight

1. Are You Actually Overweight or Just Out of Shape?
2. The Three Weight Indexes: Which Is the Best One?
3. The Exact Formula to Use

Module 3: The Perfect and Easy Diet

1. Do Calories Matter?
2. What Foods Should You Avoid?
3. What Foods Should You Eat?
4. Sample Meal Plans For the Day
5. Important Weight Loss Nutrition Your Body Needs
6. Dietary Supplements to Help You Lose Weight

Module 4: The 30-Minute Fitness Program

1. Key Exercises That You Must Do
2. How Much and How Often Should You Exercise?
3. Sample Workout Plan to Follow

Module 5: Your Personal 30-Day Plan

1. How to Create a Personalized Plan
2. Your Plan Formula
3. Sample Plan and How To Execute

Module 6: Delicious Recipes That Shed Pounds

1. Breakfast Recipes
2. Lunch Recipes
3. Dinner Recipes

4. Snack Recipes
5. Dessert Recipes

Module 7: Conclusion and Action Steps

1. Summary of Modules
2. Common Obstacles to Watch For
3. Motivational Story
4. Final Words and Action Steps

Your outline is nearly done. In fact, if you hand this to a good writer, he or she can take it from here and completely finish creating your course. The more detailed information you can give your writer, the higher quality your course will be.

So let's keep going.

TASK 3 – CREATE BULLET POINTS FOR EACH SECTION

In the last task, you broke your main modules down into three to five sections or subtopics. Now you are going to do the same thing with your sections: break each section into 3-5 bullet points as follows.

Module 3: The Perfect and Easy Diet

1. Do Calories Matter?
   • Yes! But Not In The Way You Might Think
   • Definition Of A Calorie
   • How Many Calories Does Your Body Burn In A Day
   • Should You Be Counting Calories?
   • What You Really Need To Pay Attention To

2. What Foods Should You Avoid?
   • How Certain Foods Affect Your Metabolism
   • Why You Should Avoid Dairy
   • Why You Should Avoid Gluten

3. What Foods Should You Eat?
   - So Called Super Foods And How They Affect Your Metabolism
   - Berries
   - Garlic
   - Oive Oil
   - Broccoli
   - Oats

4. Sample Meal Plans For the Day
   - Breakfast Sample Plan
   - Lunch Sample Plan
   - Dinner Sample Plan
   - Snacks Throughout The Day

5. Important Weight Loss Nutrition Your Body Needs
   - Balanced Nutrition Is Important
   - 5 Essential Nutrients For A Balanced Diet
   - Carbohydrates
   - Protein
   - Fats
   - Vitamins and Minerals
   - Water

6. Dietary Supplements to Help You Lose Weight
   - How Dietary Supplements Can Help you Lose and Maintain Your Weight
   - Caffeine
   - Green Tea Extract
   - Fish Oil

This step can also be done more easily after reviewing about five to ten top books on the same topic. This broadens your view and helps you brainstorm to make sure that you are not forgetting to include any key topics.

The ease or difficulty in writing these detailed bullet points depends on who is creating this product and his or her aptitude on the topic. You can skip

155

this task in certain cases, but it doesn't take more than 30 minutes so I do recommend my students complete it.

TASK 4 – ASSIGN MEDIA FORMATS & LENGTH

Carrying out this task myself helps me organize my thoughts and my overall project management whenever I create a course.

If you intend to do a product that is all written, this task is done in minutes and can even be skipped. However, if you plan on adding audio and video, it only takes minutes and can be very helpful when you're actually creating the product.

As always, nothing is better than an example.

Module 4:

The 30-Minute Fitness Program *(Written Introduction; 2-3 pages)*
1. Key Exercises That You Must Do *(Video; 20 minutes)*
2. How Much and How Often Should You Exercise? *(Written; 1-2pages)*
3. Sample Workout Plan to Follow *(Video; 30 minutes)*

Notice how I added (Written) or (Video) next to each topic along with a small note that indicates how long that section should be. This way when I dive in to create the product, I know exactly what to do and how to set up for it.

There you have it. If you use Amazon.com, creating your outline will be pretty fast and easy. But if you have a product already in mind, you might not even need Amazon.com.

Believe me: Once you do it for your first product, you're going to love the product outline process!

INSIDE THE CIRCLE: VIDEO BREAK #18

How To Create A Product Outline
Learn All About It Here In This Free Video:
www.lurn.com/blog/productoutline

CHAPTER 18: STEP #5
CREATING YOUR PRODUCT

Now that your outline is done, you're ready to create your product. You can either:

- Write or record it all on your own
- Outsource the whole thing
- Create parts of it yourself and outsource other parts

Most of the products offered at Lurn are built using a combination of my personally writing/filming the content plus chunks that are outsourced or done by our own staff.

Although I don't expect everyone to do the same, I believe outsourcing portions of my products has actually added value to them. Freelance websites make it simple to tap into talent and knowledge from all over the world, so it almost feels like a crime not to use outsourcing.

But, let's first discuss how to create the product yourself.

CREATING THE PRODUCT YOURSELF

There is no one right way to create a product. There are literally thousands of options, and everyone has their own unique approach.

Here are some of the techniques that have worked best for me and my Lurn Nation students. I'll also share specific strategies that allow you to create your entire course on an almost laughable budget.

There are three main types of products you can create yourself:

1. Written
2. Audio
3. Video

CREATING A WRITTEN PRODUCT

If you are going to write your own product, you don't need much equipment. Any computer with a program like Pages or Microsoft Word will be sufficient. After you finish writing, you simply export it as a PDF and you are done.

To really speed and organize your writing, simply take your outline and go one level deeper on each of the bullet points. Basically, that'll give you:

- Module Title
  - Section Title
    - Bullet Point
      - Sub-Bullet Point

When you start to detail each bullet point to this level, you will find that your course is practically writing itself!

CREATING AN AUDIO PRODUCT

When I create an audio product, I treat it as a written product; I create a deeper level outline with more bullet points, just as I would a written product. I do, however, use a more conversational writing tone so that it will sound more natural when I record it.

The only other equipment you will need is a good microphone. If this is your first product and you are just starting, you will be just fine with a good headset microphone. These can be purchased for less than $50 at your local electronics store. If you want to go more professional, I recommend investing in the Zoom HN4 which costs only $199 at the time of this writing - and is well worth the investment if you're planning to do more audio products.

It truly does not matter which microphone you use when you are just starting. When your business starts to profit and offer more cash flow, then I recommend boosting your sound with some better equipment.

Why is it OK to be so relaxed about which microphone you get? Because even the basic technology available today is almost as good as going to a professional audio studio.

Remember how easily and cost-effectively I built my own sound studio in my wife's walk-in closet? Listening to my audio products, you would seriously think that I am recording in a professional studio.

I just take my laptop into the closet, set it on a chair and hold the microphone as I read my scripted product. That's it. Nice and simple.

Most computers now come loaded with great software that will record your audio. That's one more reason why you may never need a professional audio studio again.

INSIDE THE CIRCLE: VIDEO BREAK #19

How I Use A Microphone To Easily Create Written Content

Learn More! Just Go To The Link Below:
www.lurn.com/blog/microphone

CREATING A VIDEO PRODUCT

There are four kinds of video products you can create:

1. Face to Camera
2. Screen Capture
3. Webinars and Replays
4. Scribble Pad Videos (one of my favorites)

Face to camera videos are created by setting your video camera on a level surface and recording yourself speaking to it. Working with thousands of students has taught me that many students are not comfortable in front of a video camera. If you are not comfortable in front of a camera, there is no need to put yourself through it; there are other easier options.

Pay special attention to the quality of your video and your sound. You need to have good lighting and the proper settings on the camera. If the quality of your shoot is poor, the value of your product goes down.

Personally, I use a professional video team every time I need a face to camera product video. It's a lot easier to create a high quality, high value product this way. Of course, a professional team definitely requires a good budget.

Screen capture videos are made using software on your computer simply by recording your screen and your voice. Your face never appears on the video. You can prepare PowerPoint slides ahead of time and record yourself going through them simply with your own voiceover. My students love creating these videos - probably because there is no concern about lighting or shooting quality, and virtually no editing is needed.

You can use the same microphone that you plan on using for audio products. For your screen capture, I am a big fan of two software programs:

PC = Camtasia - about $299
Mac = ScreenFlow - about $99

My ScreenFlow purchase might be one of the best investments I've ever made. I have gotten more value out of this software than I can ever explain.

Webinar and replay videos are very similar to screen-capture videos. The main difference is that you are conducting them live and recording them as well. Theoretically this allows you to start selling the product without even having made the product. You can sell customers a product that is delivered over a certain number of weeks.

In this way, you can start making sales and creating your product as you go. Products like this are often based on a PowerPoint presentation. You would use the same microphone we have already discussed, and run it all on your computer. If you use a platform like GoToWebinar to run your webinar, the software automatically records your entire webinar presentation for you.

Scribble Pad videos are where you draw and write on the screen while you narrate your presentation. They share many of the same advantages as screen capture videos. You don't have to show your face and don't need to do any fancy editing. Unlike screen capture videos, you don't need to prepare PowerPoints ahead of time. They are also more engaging to the viewer since they aren't watching a slide show.

To create Scribble Pad videos, you need a writing/drawing tablet that is compatible with your computer. I use the Wacom Intuos Pro, which costs around $300. That's only one option, you can find great Scribble Pads for as little as $99.

The Scribble Pad has been one of the best investments I've ever made. With it, along with inexpensive white board software on my computer, I am able to create easy, dynamic scribble pad lessons faster than any other type of video.

INSIDE THE CIRCLE: VIDEO BREAK #20

How I Threw Out PowerPoint & Still Created Great Video Products Without Ever Showing My Face On Camera!
HINT: I Use Something Called A Scribble Pad!
Find Out Now By Watching This Free Video:
www.lurn.com/blog/scribblepad

As you can see, creating your own product is actually very easy once your main outline is done. The outline is most of the work - and we have already covered the best resource in the world to help you quickly create the best outline possible: Amazon.com

Now, what if you do not want to create your own product? What if you want to outsource it - the way I built my initial empire? I am a big believer in the power of outsourcing, especially when you are just starting out. Outsourcing can drastically reduce your risk and your time to market - and it can even result in a higher quality product.

USING OUTSOURCING TO CREATE YOUR PRODUCT

It's impossible for me to calculate the number of times I have used outsourcing in the past 13 years. I use outsourcing on a daily basis.

With freelance websites now providing access to talent around the world - at steep international discounts - it's almost crazy not to use outside help.

I use outsourcing for many reasons:

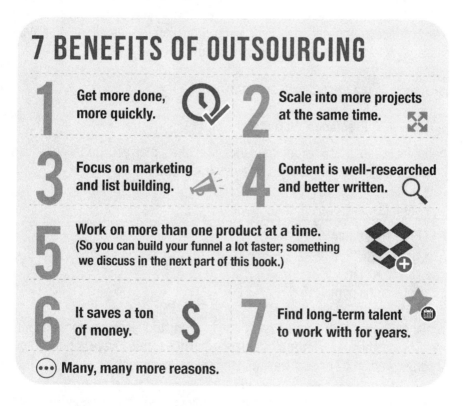

7 BENEFITS OF OUTSOURCING

1 Get more done, more quickly.

2 Scale into more projects at the same time.

3 Focus on marketing and list building.

4 Content is well-researched and better written.

5 Work on more than one product at a time. (So you can build your funnel a lot faster; something we discuss in the next part of this book.)

6 It saves a ton of money.

7 Find long-term talent to work with for years.

••• Many, many more reasons.

The first team member I ever hired started with my company as outsourced talent. The first time I ever had a technical project, I used outsourcing. The first time I ever needed a website, I used outsourcing.

I don't use outsourcing only for content creation; I use it to run many parts of my business. However, I have found it the most useful in content creation.

There are a few steps to follow to make outsourcing work well for you:

1. Choose a freelance website.
2. Post your project.
3. Choose a freelancer.
4. Manage the work output.
5. Build a strong relationship for recurring work.

The best situation results after you have spent a few months building relationships with great talent that you use over and over in your business. That's because once you find a good freelancer, you never have to post jobs or review applications. You simply fire off an email or a Skype message. A few days later, the work is done!

Here's how to get started with outsourcing:

1 – Choose A Freelance Website

There are quite a few great freelance websites that you can use. I use different ones depending on the kind of work I have.

Here are a few key ones that are popular:

• Freelancer.com
• Guru.com
• UpWork.com
• 99Designs.com

Freelancer.com is a great resource if you are looking for offshore developers. This site offers all freelance services, but I have found it best for simple and small project-based technical development.

Guru.com has been a gold mine for me to find talent that is western-based with excellent English language and grammar skills to help me create my products. The pricing for Guru vendors is more than other sites, but that is also because they feature talent from western countries.

UpWork.com is an excellent source for all-around help. UpWork also provides a lot of western-based talent for almost any kind of work. I personally spend over $50,000 a month on UpWork.com. I have found amazing talent here including programmers, content writers, personal assistants, designers... I even recently found a mechanical engineer! I highly recommend UpWork.com.

99Designs.com is an excellent resource for design projects. However, it is much more costly than any other freelance website. The greatest benefit of using 99Designs is that instead of hiring a designer blindly and hoping he or she does a good job, you can actually get several designers to do the job - and then reward only one of them the project money. That way you know exactly what you are buying before you pay for it. If you are just beginning, though, 99Designs.com may be too advanced and costly for you right now.

2 – Post Your Project

I have one major rule with posting a job on any of these sites. I take the most time I can to get as detailed as possible with my posting. I also put enough in each post to allow me to immediately know whether the freelancer actually read my post.

Many freelancers send you a private message after they bid on your work. Some of these send obviously cut-and-pasted messages to multiple job posters. To separate these freelancers from quality freelancers, I put specific details in my project post.

When posting a job description on a freelance site, hold nothing back. Take an extra day if you need to make your post as complete as possible. You'll be glad you did.

3 – Choose A Freelancer

In all my years working with freelancers, I have developed some standard rules to follow when selecting someone:

1. Never choose the least expensive or the most expensive bid. Choose somewhere in between.

2. The person must have a minimum rating of 9.5 and at least 10 projects completed on the website. I do not work with new people on the platform.

3. Always send a private message and see how fast the freelancer responds to you. I prefer those who can respond in 12 hours or less.

4. Have at least three private messages back and forth to get a good feeling for the person before making your choice.

5. Read the person's reviews - not just their star ratings. Actually go into the freelancer's profile and read what past employers have written about them. I like to pick freelancers whose past employers have left raving reviews.

Follow these simple rules, and you are likely to find someone great!

4 – Manage The Work Output

I do not believe in micro-management. However, when I bring on a new freelancer, I stay in touch on a daily basis until the project is complete. I often do the same for the next two to three projects with that freelancer as well. If the freelancer can complete at least three projects for me on time and without any issues, that is when I start to reduce my micro-management.

Initially, I use the private messaging system within the freelance website. I also use Skype to communicate with the freelancer. In rare cases, if it is a bigger project, I will get on regular phone calls as well.

When the freelancer has first started, I ask him or her to send me drafts of the work for intermittent review. To be fair, keep in mind that when someone new starts working with you, she or he doesn't know your style at first. It can definitely take a few days (or even weeks) for someone to learn your preferences.

I also stay constantly in touch so there's no chance that the person will forget about my work. Freelancers have a habit of taking on more work than they can handle. When that happens, they juggle based on which client is the loudest and most up to date. If you are constantly in touch, they will not have the opportunity to put your work on the back burner.

It is very important to make yourself available to work with your freelancer initially and to offer hands-on guidance whenever needed. Otherwise, you'll never get the quality work you want.

Although this might sound tedious, it is not that bad. It just requires you to do a check-in once a day. Once that freelancer has worked with you a few times, you can slow down on the check-ins.

5 – Build A Strong Relationship For Recurring Work

There is no better feeling than to never have to search on freelance websites; to be able to go straight to someone and assign work. Especially once this person gets to know you and your style, it really is a blessing. I would say that about 70% of the freelancers I have hired have stuck around for quite some time.

One of the benefits of having a qualifying round in the beginning is that you bring in better freelancers from the start. It gives you a better pool of candidates for future work.

When a project ends, immediately try to keep that freelancer engaged if you can. If you can work with him or her closely for at least a month or more, you will build a special relationship that gives your work priority, better rates, and speed.

Always look at your outsourced freelance projects as a way of possibly creating reliable long-term work relationships. This mentality has served me very well.

ONE LAST WORD ABOUT PRODUCT CREATION

Having trained thousands of students, I feel it's important that I take a minute to address one recurring trap in which too many students get stuck: The Perfection Trap.

Certain students never complete their product because they are too busy trying to make everything perfect. These students spend so much time trying to make the product better and better that it is never launched!

Ask yourself one question: "Is there value in this product?" If your answer is yes, then you are ready to move on to the next step. Remember, one of the brilliant things about having an online business is that you can always easily make any changes you want at any time.

Focus only on value and execution. Do not let yourself get lost in the perfection trap. Put your foot down on making changes after a certain amount of time. Even if it's imperfect, it's something.

Your goal is to get your product out there as fast as you can so you can start testing your sales message and all the other factors involved.

And remember, your main passion product is only the beginning.

If you truly want to reach $1 million, you're going to need to have more than one product. You're going to build a funnel of products. You're going to move on to the next part of the Circle of Profit where we talk about how to multiply your profits.

What does that mean? That there will be other products in your funnel that will need your time as well. Believe me: If you invest all of your time in one product, you'll end up losing bigger on the rest of it.

Once you have your passion product done, the real key to making $1 million lies in being able increase the value of each customer. In over a decade of testing and executing, I have found a very simple formula that I use to get a minimum 500% increase in my profits - without ever needing extra traffic.

The magic is in building your $1 million funnel. Ready to continue? That's what we are going to dive into in the next section!

SECTION 4 – YOUR $1 MILLION SALES FUNNEL

CHAPTER 19: HOW TO CREATE YOUR OWN $1 MILLION SALES FUNNEL

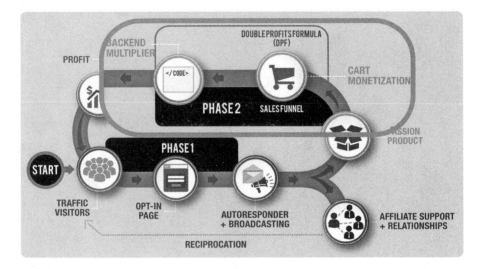

What you are about to learn in this chapter instantly added 500% growth to my business. I achieved this growth without getting a single extra visitor to my website. I did not spend an extra dime on the business. All I did was implement a very simple formula and I was able to immediately increase my 90 day customer value by 500%!

So many businesses are so focused on selling their main product that they forget about all of their other opportunities.

Here's what I mean: There are generally two kinds of online marketers. The majority are obsessed with getting more traffic to their website. Day in and day out, they go on the assumption that their business can only grow with a continual flow of more visitors.

Then there are the smart marketers. These are the marketers who focus most of their energy on increasing conversions and building stronger funnels.

And now I'd like to introduce you to the magic of the Back-End. If you're not familiar with the term, the back-end is everything that happens after a customer has already bought your main product.

Let's take a closer look.

A BRILLIANT BACK-END

Here are two terms you should know:

- Front-End - Everything it takes to get someone to buy from you.
- Back-End - Everything you market after someone buys your main product.

Your front-end represents all the work that occurs in order to get visitors to your website and to convert those visitors into purchasers. Your front-end represents your main passion product and the process of trying to sell it. I also call this the pre-transaction funnel.

Your back-end represents all the products that you can sell to your new customer. In other words: As soon as someone buys your front-end product, she or he is now a customer; the relationship has just begun - and the potential is limitless!

Your true profits actually lie in your brilliant back-end!

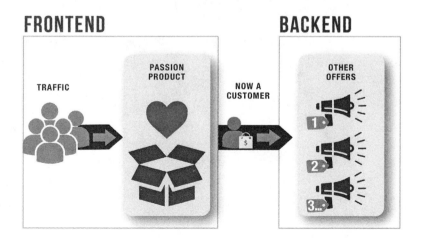

Now I'm going to show you the easiest way to build amazing offers that you can turn around very fast and profit from even faster. Let's go.

WHAT IS A SALES FUNNEL?

INSIDE THE CIRCLE: VIDEO BREAK #21

What Is A Sales Funnel And How Do Back-Ends Work?
Go Here To Watch This Free Video:
www.lurn.com/blog/salesfunnel

A sales funnel is a strategically-ordered sequence of products that you offer to your new customer as soon as he or she purchases one of your products for the first time. Typically (but not always), the price of the marketed products gets higher and the level of training and education you offer becomes more advanced and hands-on.

That's just one kind of funnel. There are unlimited combinations and kinds of funnels that you can create.

Back in Chapter 6 I showed how you, as a customer, have been an active sales funnel participant your entire life. If you recall, adding fries and a Coke to your Big Mac order means that McDonald's doubles their sale.

I love a good sales funnel. When you first walked in, McDonald's was only going to earn $3.99 from your sale. Using their classic funnel, they generated $7.27 instead.

Here's that McDonald's sales funnel diagram again:

Let's look at another example. Suppose you buy a computer at an electronics store. It costs $1,000 and the store makes a 7% profit, or $70. You are just about to check out and the sales agent behind the counter offers you a very appealing warranty. "Sir, would you like to protect your $1,000 investment for three years with our in-store warranty for only $97?" You think it could be a wise idea.

Most likely the store is partnered with a warranty company, but this time the store probably makes 75% of the sale. That means the store just made another $75 profit on your sale. They just doubled their profit!

Any strong business understands that the best customer is someone who is already a customer. If you can make additional offers to your customer when he or she has just agreed to purchase your main product, you will see a tremendous increase in your profits. We consistently see our own business and our students more than double their profits right at the shopping cart.

Just think about it. There is absolutely no risk. You never present a more advanced course or training at a higher price until your main passion product has already been sold.

These products are only sold to existing customers, which means that there is no chance to ever lose money. You can only make more. Period.

How I Instantly Scaled My Business to $3 Million

It happened way back in 2006. I was sitting in a room of marketers. We were all sharing our latest strategies and dissecting our businesses. I was very excited. I was convinced that I had amazing numbers to report. I was even convinced that I would be the star in the room.

In the 12 months before that meeting, I had generated over $1 million and was growing incredibly fast. To top it off, I had built this success from my dorm room.

I was just one marketer away from sharing my story. I was going to crush it. From all the stories that had been told, I thought mine was the best by far. My excitement was growing. Only one more person to go before it was my turn to speak.

The last marketer before me started: "I'm about to hit $3 million this year..."

I was shocked. I was even a bit heartbroken. He had just stolen my thunder! I needed to know what he had done. I was also confused because I had just spoken to this marketer a few months before and he was on track to hitting $1 million, just like I was.

How in the world did he triple his business?

The next words out of his mouth changed my business life forever. He said:

"I added an upsell after my first product, and it has drastically increased my growth rate."

By the time we met, he did not just have one upsell. He had built an entire sales funnel. He had discovered this strategy having spent over a decade in the car business. More than anyone else, he understood the power of selling your customers more services just as they are buying.

He continued his presentation on his upsell, his downsell, and what his sales funnel looked like. I was blown away.

It was time for me to go back to the drawing board.

Remarkably, I was able to implement everything he taught within just 10 days! There were four months left in the year. At my previous pace - which I thought was pretty good - I was expecting to generate about $1 million.

But in the next 10 days, I scaled my business to generate $3 million that year instead of $1 million - simply by adding a sales funnel!

CHAPTER 20: THE SECRET TO GIVING YOURSELF A 500% RAISE

Focus on your existing customers, and you will see your profits explode.

Mind you, I don't want you to slow down your traffic or your traffic acquisition strategies. But if you have to take a two-week break from your front-end to work on your brilliant back-end, I think you'll find it's an amazingly profitable investment.

To this day, I am shocked to see how many online business owners are still missing this piece of the puzzle. As a matter of fact, when I consult most online businesses, the fastest way for me to become their hero is to help them implement a sales funnel.

Let me give you an example: Recently, I was helping one of my students, Sammy. She had just launched her first passion product.

Sammy was doing great. She was hardworking and really taking action on what she was learning. She had finished the entire Lurn Nation training in less than six weeks and had already seen profits from Phase 1 in the first 14 days.

Now she was focusing on launching her own passion-based information product.

But like many digital publishers, she had completely ignored the back-end.

When it came time for me to review her business, the first thing I noticed was that we needed to add a back-end. I sent her a few presentations to watch and told her to immediately add at least one more product to her sales funnel. Sammy was able to focus and add her entire sales funnel in just three weeks.

She immediately compared her previous sales numbers to her brilliant back-end numbers. I don't have to tell you how happy she was; take a look for yourself:

Sammy's Pre- & Post- Brilliant Back End Numbers		
Phase 1		
10,342 Visitors → 6,089 Subscribers → 152 Sales at $47 =		
$7,144 Sales		
PHASE 2	No Back End	5x Brilliant Back End
Using Double Profits Formula	0	**+ $6,643 Sales** (**$3,321 Profit**)
Using Backend Multiplier	0	**+ $11,400**
PROFIT *(After Paying Affiliates)*	**$3,572**	**$18,293.50***
*That's 512% more than what she was doing before!		

Without adding even one more visitor to her website, Sammy made 512% more money - a $18,293.50 profit!

Imagine how much more investment capital she had the next month to really scale her business. And that's exactly what she did. The next month, she reinvested $10,000 of her $18,293 to get more traffic.

Guess what?

She got 21,453 visitors to her website. I'm not kidding. The scale she added was enormous. Her profits shot up and even through today, her earnings continue to grow!

All this was possible because she took three weeks to build a simple back-end.

THE TWO PARTS OF A BRILLIANT BACK-END

There are an unlimited number of ways that you can increase your profits in the back-end. Almost all of them fall into two categories:

- Double Profits Formula (DPF)
- Back End Multiplier (BM)

Your entire business can change even if you only add one of the two back-end categories to your marketing strategy.

I always tell our Lurn Nation students that they should implement these one at a time.

- First, build your double profits formula back-end.
- Second, build your back-end multiplier.

When you combine both of the back-end strategies you can see 500%+ growth in your profits. Let's look at each of these in greater detail.

CHAPTER 21: THE DOUBLE PROFITS FORMULA

The Double Profits Formula (DPF) all takes place "at cart."

What does that mean?

Imagine a visitor comes to your website and reads some sales material about your main front end passion product. He decides to make this wise investment and he completes your order page. He clicks submit and is now officially your customer.

You now have two options:

1. Send this customer to a thank you page and give him access to your product.
2. Offer the customer an opportunity to upgrade his order by adding more advanced training, usually at a higher investment.

The DPF always takes place immediately when a customer has just purchased your main product. The minute they transact with you, you can either deliver the product they purchased - or you can make an additional offer.

Marketers also call this the "at cart" process. We call it "at cart" because the customer has just bought your main product and is still at your shopping cart. The customer is still in the process of buying - his level of interest is at the highest that it may ever be.

Here's another way to understand DPF:

At a physical store, you walk in and browse the electronics section. After a few minutes, you find what you are looking for and head to the cash register.

From the time you reach that cashier to the time you walk out of the store, you are officially in DPF territory. Everything DPF takes place in this window.

But anything that happens after you buy your item and walk out the door is no longer considered part of the DPF. Now you're in Back-End Multiplier country.

Take that same example and move it online. From the time your customers enter their credit card information to the time they take delivery of their purchase, they are still "at cart."

The Double Profits Formula is what kicks off your sales funnel. It is the first step to building out your 5X Sales Funnel.

Now I'll show you what a typical "at cart" funnel looks like, and what a great DPF sales funnel looks like:

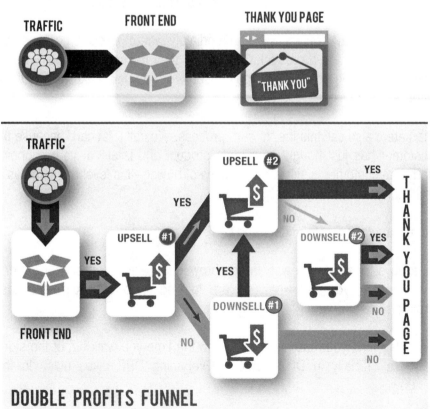

TYPICAL "BORING" SALES FUNNEL

DOUBLE PROFITS FUNNEL

INSIDE THE CIRCLE: VIDEO BREAK #22

DPF Sales Funnel Explained &
How It Doubles Your Profit
Get Started! Free Video Below To Learn More:
www.lurn.com/blog/funnelexplained

In the first example, the customer purchased the main product and that was it. They were allowed to check out and receive the product they purchased. In the DPF funnel (bottom image), you have added a tremendous amount of profit to your business. Let me walk you through this buying funnel.

Steps of the Classic DPF Funnel

Step 1 - The customer sees Upsell #1. This is the first offer for more advanced training. The customer has a choice to say YES or NO.

Step 2 - If the customer says YES and purchases this offer, you are in a great position to then offer this customer one more upgrade option, Upsell #2. However, if the customer says NO and refuses Upsell #1, you offer what we call a "downsell." (I will explain these terms in detail in the next part of this chapter). The downsell is just a less expensive offer or a discount given for the purpose of saving the sale.

Step 3 - If the customer says NO to the downsell as well, take them straight to the thank you page. If the customer has said no twice in a row, it becomes clear that the customer is done and will not currently invest any more money. At this point you stop the DPF funnel and simply give your customer access to the product they bought.

However, if the customer agrees to buy Downsell #1, you have them back in the "yes loop." You will now take the customer straight to see Upsell #2.

Step 4 - On Upsell #2, if the customer agrees and says yes, you will now consider the double profits formula to have been a huge success and take the customer to the thank you page.

THE CIRCLE OF PROFIT

However, if this customer declines Upsell #2, you again have the ability to make a save the sale offer and take the customer to Downsell #2. Whether or not you use Downsell #2 is a personal choice. It does work and it does add sales; however, compared to the rest of the sales funnel, the amount Downsell #2 adds is usually very small.

Step 5 - If the customer refuses to buy Downsell #2, you again have had two consecutive declines and it's time to take this customer to the thank you page.

Even if the customer agrees to purchase Downsell #2, you will still take that customer to the thank you page. The double profits formula will now have been a big success again.

As you can tell, it can be easy to get carried away with a sales funnel. In my 10+ years of experience using sales funnels, I have found it very wise to never offer more than two products directly in the "at cart" funnel.

You are most welcome to offer more products, but you want to do that starting a few days later. We will cover that in the upcoming back-end multiplier section.

HOW MUCH CAN A SALES FUNNEL MAKE FOR YOU?

We have to do some math in order to reveal the power of a sales funnel. Try your best to keep up because we are going to make many assumptions and use some good old multiplication and division.

Before you start, there are a couple of terms you need to understand.

Conversion. Whenever I say, "This percent converted into a sale," I am referring to the number of people who saw the sales message divided by how many of them purchased. For example, if I send 1,000 visitors to a sales page and 30 of them choose to buy, I have a conversion rate of 30 divided by 1,000, which is .03 or 3%. If 300 of them had decided to buy, I would have a conversion rate of 30%.

Price. Each of your products has its own price whether it's a main product, an upsell, or a downsell.

Now let's look at the same funnel. This time, it contains some assumptions. I have inserted price assumptions and also conversion assumptions. Please note that these numbers will be very specific to your situation and they will change drastically based on your environment, niche, marketing, messaging, and many other factors.

However, the example below is based on more than 10 years of building my own funnels and having seen hundreds of sales funnels built by my students.

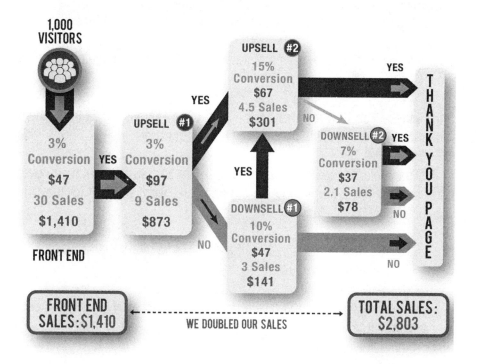

The assumptions above are very conservative. I have actually been able to see far better results as I mastered the double profits formula.

There are two kinds of conversion data in this diagram.

The front-end conversion is only 3% because this will always be your lowest converting product. After all, it is being shown to website visitors who are coming to your website only out of curiosity.

The back-end conversions are showing much larger numbers, as high as 30%. These numbers are much higher because these sales are calculated against your actual customers - not site visitors. With your front-end conversion, we used 1,000 visitors as our audience number. For the backend conversions, we are only using the number 30 - the visitors who ended up becoming customers.

Always remember that in most cases, your first upsell will always be higher converting because that is where you have the most attention from your new customer. They just gave you their credit card number, after all!

You can see that we are making a chunk of profit at each stage of the sales funnel.

Each number on its own may not be incredibly impressive. But add them up. You will quickly see that you just doubled your profit.

In this particular diagram, you earned an extra $1,393 for free. You never had an extra visitor and you never did any extra work - except for the time you took to set up this funnel.

Not bad at all! Now it's time you start getting some awesome ideas on how to build your own sales funnel.

A sales funnel (during the DPF stage) is comprised of only two elements that are easy to master:

• Upsells
• Downsells

In the next chapter, I am going to make you a complete upsell and downsell business pro!

CHAPTER 22: UPSELLS AND DOWNSELLS

Upsells are simple. During the time that your customer is still in your shopping cart, any product that you offer is considered an upsell. When you buy your computer at the local electronics store and they offer you an extended warranty, they are upselling you.

Here is another example.

Assume that you are selling a product that teaches people how to invest in the stock market. Your main product is priced at $97. It is a written and audio course that teaches your three specific secrets to making millions in the stock market.

Time to think of an upsell.

You have several options when you are creating upsells. If you stick to any of these methods, you should be able to come up with excellent ideas for almost any product.

FAST OPTIONS TO CREATE UPSELLS

There are unlimited ways to create a valuable upsell. The following list is just a small sample to help get your creative juices flowing.

1. Advanced Material

Advanced material is one of the easiest ways to create an upsell. For example, perhaps in your stock-investing course, one of the three secrets is the most important. You may also think that this one secret is so great that it deserves its own course if someone really wants to master it.

You could simply create an additional, more detailed and advanced course on just that one strategy. In this case, let's say your main course is 300 pages, and you are covering the entire topic of stock investing. Your upsell course might also be 300 pages, but this time it will be all about that single secret.

This strategy is fast, simple, and converts very well for customers who just bought your course.

2. Different Form of Media

Often, people choose to use written or audio media as their main product. If this is the case, then you already have an extremely easy upsell half done for you. In our investing course example, assuming the course is written and audio, you could simply take the same content and make a video course as well.

Perhaps being on video will allow you to get into some more advanced techniques. Students often find it easier to learn with video, so they are willing to pay more for it.

3. LIVE Training or Coaching Series

Using "LIVE Training" is one of my favorite forms of upsells. But when I say "LIVE," I do not mean being on a stage with people sitting in front of you.

Thanks to the Internet, there are very simple automated technologies that allow you to run real-time webinar conferences. All you need is a PowerPoint presentation and some notes, and you can run LIVE virtual teaching sessions.

In our example, you could create a six-week investing boot camp where you personally get on a live webinar with a small group of customers. You then delve into each strategy in your course and personally teach, get more advanced, even conduct a question-and-answer session.

When you offer LIVE training or coaching, you can easily raise the price into the hundreds and no one will blink an eye.

Taking this concept further, you only have to do this six-week boot camp once. You can actually build the upsell product as you go, adding more content each week.

Once you have taught your first group of students, during the first six weeks, you can take the webinar recordings and put them into the members area.

Perfect. You get the added perceived value of a LIVE training upsell. You can build it as you go, saving you a lot of time to launch. On top of that, you never have to repeat it; you can just record it once and you're done for the life of that sales funnel.

You can start to see now why I absolutely love using this upsell idea.

4. Software

Software programs are truly some of the best upsells. I do not personally use them very much because I am not a technical person. I do not like the thought of getting software developed. I have always been known as the "education guy." I like selling content and information.

However, when having a software upsell made sense, I did try it. The results were amazing. There is no better sales pitch than to tell a new customer, "Hey, you are about to learn exactly how to invest in the stock market using my three hidden secrets, but if you are in a rush, why not just skip the learning and let my software do it all for you, in just a few clicks?"

Read that pitch again. Heck, even I'm sold!

Software can sell very well. The key is that you have to have software at your disposal and that it has to fit your market. For example, if you are teaching men how to talk to women, software probably is not going to be the right upsell product for you!

5. Horizontal Expansion

Here is your savior if the previous four ideas do nothing to spark any ideas. Horizontal expansion upsells offer products in complementary niches and topics to yours, rather than products which are more advanced or deeper versions of your main product.

Using our investing niche example, your upsell could be an entire course on how to use mutual funds to safely build long-term wealth. Do you see what we did there?

We did not position an upsell around the stock-investing topic. We offered a new - but related - topic: Mutual fund investing. Anyone interested in stock investing would also have an interest in mutual fund investing. By doing this, you are simply repeating the steps in Section 3 and creating another product.

DOWNSELLS

Downsells are simple.

There are two approaches to creating a downsell. Both approaches require almost no change to the actual upsell product.

So, what exactly is a downsell? A downsell comes up when your customer declines an upsell. Almost 95% of the time, you will find that the customer declined the offer because he did not want to spend more money, or he felt that the upsell product was too expensive.

This is when we deploy the downsell. A downsell is a final attempt to change your customer's mind by addressing their main concern: Price.

For years now, I use a standard rule with downsells. I reduce the price by 50%. If the upsell is $97, then the downsell becomes $47. If the upsell is $47, it becomes $27.

You get the idea.

Combining a major price decrease with the possibility that this will be the last chance to ever get this product usually does the trick.

You do not need to recreate a new product. You can still sell the same upsell product with just a few tweaks such as:

Remove some of the bonuses. Assuming you had added three to five bonuses to convince your customer to buy the upsell, you could remove a couple of these from the offer to justify cutting the price by 50%.

Do not change the product at all. Just give a one-time only, last opportunity at 50% off. Now, some marketers feel this is unfair to the original customers who paid the full price for the upsell; some don't. Personally, I like to remove a few bonuses to make sure the price drop is justified. You can do it either way, based on your own preferences.

If you don't want to do a 50% discount or remove bonuses, you have another option: A payment plan. I have been deploying this strategy lately for my more expensive upsells and it has worked very well.

Assuming you have a $247 upsell, you can offer the customer three payments of $97 each. This way, the perceived price (what he has to pay instantly) is cut by more than 50%. But you don't have to make any changes - and the downsell is more than justified.

That's it. Downsells are so simple; there really is nothing more to it.

There you have it. The double profits formula (DPF) really is that easy. This is why so many of our Lurn Nation students are able to fully implement it in a matter of days and can easily double their profits and the profits that their affiliates make.

Of course, the more profits you make, the more you can invest in getting more traffic and feed your Circle of Profit!

Let's continue now with the 5X Profit Secrets model and a strategy I call the Back End Multiplier. This is going to be your secret weapon in achieving $1 million, and it's your final step to completing the Circle of Profit.

CHAPTER 23: BACK-END MULTIPLIER –
THE FINAL FRONTIER TO YOUR $1 MILLION

Imagine that you've bought a new home. Two weeks after you move in, your home builder sends you a letter offering you free interior design services. You think to yourself, "Wow, that is just what I need - and it's free!" You take him up on it.

When the interior designers come to your house, they suggest particular styles of furniture and accessories for your new home. They also recommend a few select retailers who offer these items.

The truth is that the home builder will be making a commission from all of the purchases you make. The interior designers' compensation comes from the stores they recommend.

Sounds a lot like affiliate marketing, does it not?

Envision another picture: I recently purchased a Mac Pro computer from Apple. Within days of my purchase, I began receiving emails from Apple telling me about its amazing Cinema Display monitor. Then I started receiving stronger sales emails with offers on the product; not just one, but more than one. After all, my Mac Pro can support up to six of these monitors. Each of these costs $997.

If you come to my office today, you will see three Cinema Display monitors on my desk. Apple was able to turn my $3,000 purchase (the Mac Pro) into a $6,000 purchase - by selling me three more Cinema Displays.

Had Apple not sent me emails educating me on the value of its Cinema Display, I would have bought much less expensive generic monitors. I might also have been unhappy with my purchase and post-purchase experience. Sounds kind of like an upsell, right? The difference is that it happened after I had left the store.

This brings us to the Back End Multiplier. A back end multiplier is anything that you endorse or sell to your customer after they have left your shopping cart.

A back end multiplier can happen a day after the purchase, or (my personal favorite) two weeks later.

There are two types of back end multipliers.

1. High Ticket Affiliate Offer. This is your endorsement of a higher ticket ($497+) offer from someone else. You run an email campaign promoting the product only to your customers, usually 10-14 days after they have become customers.

2. High Ticket Upsell. This is your email campaign to sell your own product, training, coaching, live event, or workshop. Whatever product you create, it should carry immense value and be something you sell for at least $497, although this number can vary based on your niche.

I do incredibly well with both of these strategies. I like to start with my own high-ticket upsell. That way, I don't have to share affiliate commissions with anyone. Then, about two weeks later, I promote a high-ticket affiliate offer.

It's important to note my frequent use of the term "high-ticket" here.

If you want to make more profit, it is very important that your back-end multiplier has a $497 or higher price point (again, this number can vary based on your niche). Remember: You are now marketing to individuals who are proven buyers. You will make a lot more money by making a higher ticket offer.

Remember Sammy, the Lurn Nation student who was about to skip the brilliant back-end strategy and push forward with only her passion product? Sammy was able to create an extra $11,400 in pure profit simply by using both a high ticket affiliate offer and her own high ticket offer. All she had to do was promote these items to her existing customers within the first month of their purchases.

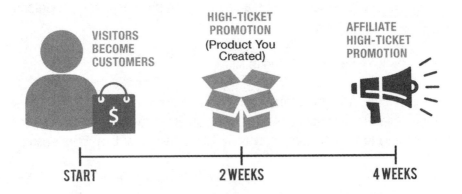

The process of creating your high ticket offers is no different from what we discussed in Section 2. You do, however, have to get more intimate and more advanced.

CHAPTER 24: PUTTING IT ALL TOGETHER

As you can see, from the day you get your first subscriber to the day you create your backend multiplier is all a part of the same circle. If you want to turn your passion into $1 million, you are going to need to not only follow but master each of these steps. I have spent over 10 years mastering this system and have trained thousands of students.

I have dedicated my life to Lurn because I see too many talented people in this world who are miserable in their lives and unhappy in their financial situation - when they absolutely do not need to be.

I firmly believe that your talents, passions, hobbies, and expertise are gifts that you need to share with the world. And you never need to share these gifts without also being able to create full financial freedom for yourself.

At Lurn Nation, we have a full team of coaches and a very strategic training schedule. We will take you from where you are today to where you dream of being in just a few weeks. The process is simply a series of steps - and the key is to follow these steps exactly.

No matter where you are in life, or what step you're working on, at Lurn Nation we've seen it all. We are ready to help you - and even to hold your hand through the process.

So I want to personally invite you to join Lurn.com. We have many options to fit your current situation and we're more than happy to help you discover your best potential.

What you have seen in this book is a fraction of the whole picture. The amount of hand-holding and step-by-step coaching that we offer you is like nothing you have ever seen before.

If you want to start building your business, your next best step is to visit us at www.Lurn.com. I also encourage you to very closely watch our FREE blog at: www.Lurn.com/blog.

Our mission is simple. We want to create 1,000 successful digital publishers in the world. Every day, the entire team at Lurn is truly dedicated to your success.

Now, through the four sections you've just read, you've got a great idea on what it takes to turn your passion into $1 million and how simple it can be. In the next section, we'll go over what your exact next steps are. I also want to tell you where to get absolutely free training on how you can market your new passion products.

What if you could generate your $1 million in the next 4 to 6 months? Let me show you how to do that!

SECTION 5 – THE FINAL STEPS TO $1 MILLION

Whew! We have been through quite a journey together. I want to take a moment to summarize it all.

There is also one last missing piece: The piece that allows you to enter any niche on the Internet and create $1 million within six months or less. Of course, everyone works at his or her own pace. But a million dollars in six months has been achieved by many, and if you follow the system exactly, step-by-step, it can be achieved by you as well.

The bulk of your time is spent creating the valuable products that make up your funnel. You can choose to make those products yourself, or you can outsource the entire process for pennies on the dollar.

The beauty of the Circle of Profit is that there is no one perfect way of using it. It's a very flexible system. You can tweak it to your own preferences as you wish. This section is just about that.

We are going to review each part of the circle. I'll give you an estimated timeline so you know exactly what to expect and when. Finally, I'll give you the six-month plan that I've used multiple times myself to create $1 million over and over.

CHAPTER 25: YOUR BUSINESS PLAN FOR $1 MILLION IN 6 MONTHS

Let's start right at the beginning.

PHASE 1 – BUILDING YOUR AUDIENCE STARTING TO PROFIT

Phase 1 is quick to start and very simple. The goal of this phase is to choose your niche and start building your subscriber list. You can then use automated technology to send valuable content to your list via email.

You can start this phase in less than one hour per day.

The purpose of this phase to get you to start building subscribers so that you will have an existing group of buyers ready when you launch Phase 2. If this step truly intrigues you the most, I recommend you look into our Inbox Blueprint program (www.InboxBlueprint.com). We offer a tremendous suite of technology, training, and coaching to help you get your Phase 1 business up and running fast.

Let's review the key elements to successfully executing Phase 1.

1. Traffic

Reasonable Time to Expect: Starts within 24 hours

Any business on the Internet needs website visitors. We have created a simple click-by-click system that you can copy and paste. As long as you follow the few steps, you will have more traffic than you know what to do with.

Each niche topic is different. Different traffic sources will work better in some niches than others. Lurn's world-class experts specialize in every form of traffic you can imagine.

We have hand-selected our coaches, teachers and experts – masters in all different forms of traffic generation. We want to make sure you too become a master of all of the following:

1. Email Media
2. Google
3. Facebook
4. Bing
5. Yahoo!
6. Display Advertising
7. Social Media
8. Forum Marketing
9. Search Engine Optimization
10. Many more

2. Opt-In Page

Reasonable Time to Expect: Maximum 3 days to build (or less than 60 minutes with our technology)

This is the quickest way to capture subscribers. Your opt-in page makes a free offer in order to get your site visitors to give you their email address. You can start making hundreds of thousands of dollars with only a one-page website: An opt-in page.

The opt-in page is the highest converting type of page on the Internet. It is also the easiest to make. Lurn even has simple technology that you can use to create yours.

INSIDE THE CIRCLE: VIDEO BREAK #23

Learn How To Launch Your Email Business In Less Than 60 Minutes Using Our Click-Click Technology – FREE DEMO!
www.lurn.com/blog/freedemo

3. Autoresponders and Broadcasting

Reasonable Time to Expect: 2-3 days to fully set up, then 20-30 minutes a day after that (60 minutes using Inbox Blueprint technology)

As you build subscribers, you are going to begin communicating with them. Autoresponders and broadcasting are built specifically to handle these communications with ease. You simply log in, type an email, and it automatically goes out to all your subscribers.

We have discussed the many kinds of autoresponders currently on the market, recommended one you should use, and showed you how to get a free account with www.Sendlane.com. We also detailed the different styles of emails that you will need to write and send to your subscribers. If you decide to join Lurn Nation, you can easily start using our proven templates.

Believe it or not, that's it for Phase 1. Quick, right?

Phase 1 is quick - but it's also critically important, so we've got some incredible tricks to make it ten times easier and faster. We want to help you get through Phase 1 without a glitch so that you can get to the real profits and financial freedom waiting for you in Phase 2.

INSIDE THE CIRCLE: VIDEO BREAK #24

How To Get The #1 Autoresponder For Free For 30 Days SendLane – Claim Your Exclusive Bonus!
Learn More! Just Go To The Link Below:
www.lurn.com/blog/sendlanetrial

PHASE 2 – ROLLING YOUR WAY TO $1 MILLION

If you are more interested in developing your own information product, I would like to refer you to our Publish Academy program. This program was created and specifically designed to hold your hand through the entire process of building your own information product.

INSIDE THE CIRCLE: VIDEO BREAK #25

- -

Get A Free Tour Of Our Publish Academy Training...
Go Here To Watch This Free Video:
www.lurn.com/blog/publishacademy

---

4. Your Passion Product

Reasonable Time to Expect: 3-4 weeks from planning to completion
After you have confirmed that you have chosen a profitable passion product, you'll follow a simple series of steps to create your own highly valuable training product. This product will be your presence on the Internet. You will begin to easily market this product and instantly double the profits you are making from Phase 1.

Your passion product can be either written, audio, video, or a mix of all three. You can easily master the production of all three media. Creating each requires only a small budget and normal household items.

We also teach you precisely how to outsource some or all of the process if that's your preference.

5. Double Profits Formula (DPF)

Reasonable Time to Expect: 2-3 weeks from planning to completion
Ideally, you will create the products needed for the double profits formula at the same time you create your passion product. The double profits formula requires at least two additional products (with additional bonuses) that are part of your shopping cart funnel.

This means that as soon as your customer purchases your passion product, before gaining access to that product, you offer one or two opportunities to upgrade the order. An example of such an offer could be for the customer to purchase your advanced training.

It is consistently proven that this strategy alone will double your profits. If you were making $100 per customer, you can instantly start making $200. If done using our system, it should never take more than 3-4 weeks - and you can build it while you are building your passion product.

6. Back-End Multiplier

Reasonable Time to Expect: 1-2 weeks from planning to completion
This is the major profit-generating opportunity that many online businesses miss out on. About 1-2 weeks after your customer purchases your passion product, you promote a high-value, high-ticket offer costing $497 or more.

There are two kinds of high-ticket offers I almost always promote to my customers:

1. My Own High-Ticket Offer
2. An Affiliate High-Ticket Offer

I usually create a more intimate training program with more personal access to me or my top trainers and price it at $497 or above. This offer seriously boosts my profit margins, especially considering I do not have to pay any affiliate commissions on it.

About two weeks after promoting my own high-ticket offer, I position a high-ticket affiliate offer. This means the entire offer is owned by someone else and I am simply promoting it as an affiliate. Given the higher price, I make large commissions without adding any work to my day.

All of these strategies together give me a 500% boost in profits, allowing me to scale my business faster.

7. Profits

Reasonable Time to Expect: Within 1 week of Phase 1 launch
Profits are, of course, what this is all about! You should start seeing some profits very early in the process with just your email list. The major jump in profits will come once you start creating your own products and funnels.

Remember, in order to scale larger, you have to reinvest a portion of your profits back into your business religiously every month. Invest in more traffic, more training, more products... all of it. The more you follow our system to invest your profits in the right places, the easier you will fly past your $1 million goal!

And there you have it.

That is the Circle of Profit: Amazingly simple - yet completely revolutionary.

I want you to keep learning this profit-making system even more by joining me and continuing on this path to lifelong financial freedom. The more we work together, the more you will learn the amazing shortcuts and secrets to make your journey far easier and 10 times faster.

This is just the beginning of our journey together. I've invested 13 years of my life into this program, and all I ask is that you go through it all, one step at a time.

CHAPTER 26: QUICK CHECKLISTS
TO KEEP YOU ORGANIZED

As you get ready to start your passion business, the following list is going to be very helpful. Remember, if you are serious, you need to continue your training, and we can really help guide you the entire way. You can even get a hands-on coach and mentors (who have done it themselves) to guide you.

Each of these steps is taught in great detail with video tutorials. To start, be sure to head over to www.Lurn.com.

Phase 1: Entering and Dominating the Email Marketing World

1. Choosing your niche
2. Creating a Free Gift
3. Finding an affiliate offer for your TYP (Thank You Page)
4. Build your Opt-in Page and write copy based on your Free Gift
5. Research affiliate offers for your autoresponder series
6. Write a series of 10 autoresponder emails. Use a combination of promotional, content and relationship emails. Remember your first email should deliver the Free Gift you promised on the Opt-in page.
7. Send Traffic to your Opt-in Page

Phase 2: Launching Your Passion Product

1. Confirm Niche (Use the specific formula taught to assure profitability)
2. Research Top 5-10 Products in Same Niche/Topic
3. Create Product Outline
4. Create Product (or have it outsourced)
5. Sales Material - Written or Video (Taught in great detail inside Publish Academy; template samples provided as well)
6. Decide on Double Profits Formula Sales Funnel
7. Upsell #1
8. Downsell #1
9. Upsell #2
10. Downsell #2

11. Decide on Back End Multiplier
12. High-Ticket Offer
13. Affiliate High-Ticket Offer
14. Create Products For Brilliant Back End (Above)
15. Test Entire Funnel (More on This Below)

As you can see, if you are truly dedicated, it does not have to take long at all before you can turn your passions into great profits. If you're ready to start right away, all you need to do is follow the Circle of Profit and the simple steps that our system gives you.

CASE STUDY: MY PERSONAL $1 MILLION SNOWBALL LAUNCH — HOW I CREATED MY OFFER: FUTURE OF WEALTH

By now, you know the basic story of how I started learning the secrets to successful online marketing back in 2004. I never meant to become an expert in entrepreneurship or online marketing. I wanted to be in the personal development niche; that was my main passion.

But I got so good at online marketing and at attracting students that eight years later, online marketing was still my main business.

And in 2012, when I was seeing my worst days in business, I made myself a promise: "When I climb out of these dark days, I will publish my first product on just how I did it. I will teach the world all the strategies I have used to save my life and save my wealth."

So in early 2013, after I had dug myself out of debt and reclaimed my wealth, I knew it was time to make good on my promise. In one night I created the entire outline of my steps to success. The entire course just seemed to pour out of me. I never hired an outsourcer. Not for this product.

I called one of my best friends. He brought his camera and lights and we set up a video studio using $300 flip-cams and table lamps for lighting.

We shot the entire course in my apartment in India, using regular home flip-cams. And this product went on to generate millions of dollars.

The entire outline and product took me less than two weeks to create. Once the passion bug bit me, I was really working fast and was truly focused.

As I finished my main product, I reviewed the outline to evaluate what might be missing. What else could I add to the product to make it even better? Based on what I discovered, I created more outlines. These would become additional upsells for my funnel, plus some bonuses that I would give away for free.

Again, between using the built-in free microphone on my laptop and a $300 flip camera, I was back to creating the remainder of the products for my funnel. (Today you can do it all with just your iPhone.)

In less than 30 days, I had achieved my lifelong dream. My first entire personal development product was complete, and it was amazing. I was very proud of what I had created. And I knew that with it, I would be changing lives.

But here was my big problem: I did not know anything about how to market in this niche.

You might be thinking the same thing: "Anik, I can create the product fine, but how will I sell it?"

Well, even though I had eight years of marketing experience, I did not know a single person in the personal development niche. It was as if I was starting from the very beginning.

I turned to the Circle of Profit, and I began to build my funnel... and then it was time for a "snowball launch."

What's a snowball launch, you ask?

In the next chapter, we are going to dissect the process of taking a new niche and turning it into $1 million the way I did in the personal development market.

We have spent a great deal of time discussing the mechanics of turning your passion into $1 million. There is just one main topic left: How exactly do you launch this new product - and your brilliant back-end sales funnel - to your market? How do you turn your amazing new products into easy profits?

That's next.

CHAPTER 27: THE SNOWBALL LAUNCH – ROLLING YOUR WAY TO $1 MILLION

I call it the snowball launch.

The snowball launch can be broken down into three phases:

1. Testing
2. Power of One
3. Official Announcement

These three phases can take as long as you want. However, if you follow our system exactly, each of them should be relatively short.

Here's an introduction to each of the three snowball launch phases.

1. Testing

Once you have finished your passion product and your sales funnel, and everything is ready to go, it is time to test the process.

You are testing for two main parameters:
- Technically: Does it work?
- Sales Conversions: Is it converting well?

We have not discussed the simple technology aspects yet.

Before you can start aggressively getting traffic, you need to do a test order to make sure everything is working. Then, as long as your technical processes are working, you can test your sales conversions.

This testing requires a small amount of investment traffic, typically with as little as $300. The key to remember is that if you have followed our instructions exactly, you are not really risking any money.

You will earn that money back very fast because with your own products, you are making a 100% profit. You are also getting a lifetime customer.
I always recommend you start slowly and scale prudently. But any investment you make now in traffic testing is very safe.

CASE STUDY (CONTINUED): HOW I CONFIRMED THAT MY FIRST PERSONAL DEVELOPMENT PRODUCT WAS A WINNER

I had created my first personal development program: Future of Wealth. So how exactly did I begin generating traffic and sales for this new product?

When it came time to launch my product, I had to first test it.

Step 1 – I sent an email to my own list.

Promoting a product to your own email list will always lead to better conversions than any other form of marketing. If your numbers are low with this traffic group, then your sales material very probably needs to be reworked.

Step 2 – I invested $500 in email media.

This was a great move because I immediately made $600; I was able to profit on my test traffic! If you are looking for a great resource to get excellent quality and safe email media traffic, I recommend the www.Clickonomy.com traffic network.

Step 3 – I invested $1,000 in more email media.

Again, I recovered my investment and more by generating $1,500 in the first 24 hours. I continued to improve my processes with the data I was collecting.

Step 4 – I invested $500 in Facebook traffic.

With Facebook I was able to generate $750. Again, I profited. My numbers were looking great and I knew I was ready to take it to the next step; it was time for the "Power of One" to kick in.

I now started to attract other marketers to promote my product in exchange for a commission. This is absolutely risk-free traffic!

You should not start scaling your traffic before testing and having as much data as possible. You especially never want to use the "Power of One" strategy until you are at least 90% sure that your entire funnel is converting very well.

The main thing is to ensure that your funnel is converting well enough for your affiliates who, as you know already, are other marketers who promote your product for free, only earning a commission when they generate a sale for you.

2. Power of One

The Power of One might be one of the greatest marketing tools you ever have in your business. This one strategy alone has saved my life many times.

- It helped start my business in 2005.
- It helped grow my business to $10 million in 2008.
- It helped save my business in 2012.
- It helped me launch into my true passion niche in 2013.
- It helped me build an empire training for entrepreneurs in 2014.

The best part is that my students are using the Power of One every single day with as much success as I - if not more!

RITOBAN'S STORY: FROM $300/MONTH TO $1 MILLION

This is the story of a student who has now become one of my closest friends. He sent me an email one day from India. He wanted to learn how to release his own product on the Internet.

Now, I get a lot of emails and unfortunately I cannot respond to them all.

But something in his email made me stop in my tracks: He was from the same small city as my family. I had never met any marketer or student from there, so I responded.

After college, he had worked at a job making $300 a month - about what any new college graduate earns as full time income in India. But Ritoban wanted more for himself.

So he spent night and day studying online marketing. Using affiliate marketing, he started making over $10,000 a month. Naturally, he quit his job.

But he still wanted more. That was why he sent me an email. He said he wanted to get to the next level.

For the next six weeks, all I did was help him through Phase 2 of the Circle of Profit system. Less than 100 days after sending me an email, he had generated his first $1 million online.

His life has never been the same, and you'll learn more about him in the next chapter.

So, where does the Power of One come into play?

Well, the day he first emailed me, he was putting the Power of One into play for his own business - without even knowing it.

It was that day that I became his Power of One. He only needed one person (me) and I was able to make all the perfect connections for him to go on and pull off a launch that generated his business $1 million!

The Power of One proves that you need to have only ONE good contact or affiliate in any niche and you can take it over. Even if you are entering into a niche and do not know anyone, I am going to show you how to find at least one person who will respond to your email, like I did for Ritoban.

It is not hard. Seriously, it is just a numbers game.

If you use my system exactly to send out at least 10 emails or Skype chats, I will bet my left pinky finger that at least one person will respond to you. That's it. Congratulations. Nurture that one relationship the way I teach you, and you will be well on your way to your first $1 million.
The way that the Power of One works is that just one person is enough to create a viral network for you. This one person will be able to test promoting your product as an affiliate. This one person will become a friend.

You will take great care of that One. You will make sure that when that One promotes your product, the One gets excellent results and conversions.

Remember, an affiliate is someone who will send you traffic and you will, in turn, give that person a commission (50-75%). By the way, this is why I preach about testing an offer first. You want to make sure before going into this Power of One relationship that you have no risk on the table.

Here is how the viral element begins.

As soon as this person finishes promoting your product, you take their results and report the results back to them.

Assuming the results are stellar and this person is happy with them, you simply ask them to introduce you to at least three other friends on Skype or email.

Remember, if someone has been in this niche for some time, they will know a lot of other people in that niche, too.

I have seen my students use the Power of One in many niches. From Internet marketing and investing to personal development and even the dating market; I have witnessed the Power of One launch massive businesses that tower past $1 million!

CASE STUDY (CONTINUED): HOW THE POWER OF ONE HELPED ME TO MEET THE TOP MARKETERS IN PERSONAL DEVELOPMENT

I had the product. I had the funnel. I had even tested my offer. Now, I just needed to make some major moves to get to $1 million as fast as possible. I decided to use the Power of One... but I used it three times, not just once.

Power of One #1: In order to test my funnel, I had been buying email media from three different marketers. This means I was consistently buying personal- development clicks from marketers to market my product. In the process of doing this, I began to have a lot of conversations with the sellers.

I became friends with these marketers. Because I was consistently buying advertising for my product, they became interested in how well my product was converting. As they saw my results coming in, they started to refer me to their friends. All I had to do was ask them for a few introductions.

Not one of them said no. They were happy to introduce me to everyone they could.

Power of One #2: Before I finished creating my Future of Wealth product, I had been practicing Phase #1 and had built up an email list of nearly 10,000 subscribers. During this time there was one particular affiliate offer I promoted very aggressively, and I was making most of my income with it.

Of course, I had made the owner of the offer thousands of dollars as well. I reached out to him. In less than eight hours we were talking on Skype and he had already connected me to five of his top affiliates!

Power of One #3: Using one of the connections I had made from my previous Power of One, I got invited to a personal development mastermind event. I hopped on the plane and spent three days with some of the top marketers in personal development.

Of course, there was no better place to meet people, and I focused all my energies on one of the main marketers there. He and I went out to lunch together and really hit it off. He pledged his support. He told me he would make sure I met everyone in the space.

I didn't know if I should believe him, but I was excited. Sure enough, just seven days later, he sent out more than 65 personal introduction emails for me!

The contacts I made from his introductions have helped to make me millions of dollars. The Power of One is powerful.
You can be shy. You can be an introvert. It doesn't matter. The Power of One can be fully activated from behind your computer, using nothing but digital tools.

3. Official Announcement

Once your network grows and your funnel testing proves successful, you will officially announce your launch. At this point, you are going to aggressively seek other affiliates to send you traffic in exchange for a commission.

Putting together a product launch is an art in and of itself. The full product launch process reaches outside the scope of this book. However, our Lurn Nation students are taught every detail and go on to get massive results.

If you use the Power of One correctly, the official product announcement will start itself. Your main tasks are to pick a period of time and to provide prizes for your affiliates.

For instance, let's say you declare a window of three weeks and convince your affiliates to promote during that window. During that time you run a contest for your affiliates to win cool prize giveaways in exchange for their support.

You will be shocked at how differently affiliates react to you when you give them a designated period of time in which they need to send their email. The key is to make sure that you have fully tested the offer and that you are happy with the results.

CASE STUDY (CONTINUED): MY PERSONAL $1 MILLION SNOWBALL LAUNCH — THE FINAL KEY TO MY $1 MILLION LAUNCH

I used the Power of One to have at least ten different affiliates promote my product for me. They all had excellent results. These affiliates were even excited to promote my product to other affiliates. They were happy to connect me to anyone I asked for.

I chose a launch window that was one month long, and put together a superb list of contest prizes.

My affiliates are all friends with each other, but they are also very

213

competitive. Going into the official product launch, I already had nearly 1,000 sales for my product, through my testing campaigns and the ten affiliates who had helped me test by promoting.

By the time my one-month launch was over, I had over 10,000 sales.

That is the kind of power a good product launch can bring to your income. I surpassed my $1 million goal with flying colors during that one-month period. The best part is that the entire funnel and everything was already done. During that one-month period, I never did anything other than simply contact affiliates.

Every affiliate I contacted was through the Internet. Every affiliate I contacted was introduced to me by a friend. I never cold-called or "sold" anyone. Because of the warm introductions, almost every person I met was very welcoming.

I had gone from not knowing anyone in the entire personal development niche to knowing almost everyone. I did it all using Skype and Facebook. I did it in less than 60 days.

Since that launch, I have consistently generated more than $1 million on every product I release. I have a long list of great friendships and affiliates to rely on for any product I release.

I should also add that because of all the traffic these affiliates sent me, my Phase 1 income went through the roof. I built an email list of over 100,000 subscribers and have since been able to rely on more than $1 million a year in affiliate income - on top of the income I make from my own products.

It's powerful stuff.

Once the Circle of Profit starts feeding itself, it never stops.

CHAPTER 28: A MESSAGE FROM ONE OF MY TOP STUDENTS, NOW RUNNING A MULTI-MILLION DOLLAR ORGANIZATION

When one of my top students found out that I was writing this book, he insisted on writing a message for you. Of all the students I've had, his results truly are the most inspiring. I have rarely seen the kind of determination he has shown.

You read about him earlier in this book. His name is Jimmy Kim, and he works hard. He lives his life to the fullest. He fights for his dreams.

Most of all, he really puts the Circle of Profit into full use. He fuels his Circle every single day.

Jimmy is also one of my best friends. He started using the exact system behind the Circle of Profit a little over five years ago. The results he achieved are absolutely awe-inspiring.

In 2015, he is well on his way to generating over $10 million in online sales.

In the words of Jimmy Kim:

> "You have to believe in yourself and you have to take action. Anybody can do this.
>
> I used to work very hard. I am talking over 16-hour days. I started my career washing cars at a dealership. I showed a lot of dedication and in just a few years, I worked my way up to the top management in that same dealership. As great as that was, it also meant waking up by 6 am and not getting back home until 11 pm.
>
> Even when I made good money, I barely had time to enjoy it. I did this for years and years and I could not take it anymore. I was so exhausted and the thought of doing that for the rest of my life made me stay up all night.

That was when I came across Anik and his training. Honestly, I never believed it initially. How could someone make millions of dollars just sitting at home? If this was really possible, why wasn't everyone doing it? I lived in doubt for quite some time. Then, one day, I just couldn't take the day-to-day grind any more and I decided to go out on a limb and try what Anik was talking about. I have to tell you, I was immediately hooked.

Not only did it work, but it worked fast.

Within the first 30 days, I was in profit. Within the first 90 days, I was making the same income I had made in my full-time management job.

Now, understand this: It had taken over six years to get my management job. Here I was able to get to the same income in just three months. Imagine: Six years versus three months.

That was it. From there, I never looked back. My first year as an online entrepreneur following the Circle of Profit system, I was able to generate over $250,000. The problem is, I was still being a bit lazy. I never released my own product. I generated $250,000 by only using Phase #1.

Then, my second year, I decided to get serious. I got involved with product development, and my income that year jumped straight to $1 million. This is profit, by the way; that is what I actually earned.

My third year, I continued to grow. I entered new niches. I released more products and made new partnerships using the Circle of Profit. My income continued to grow and I continued to launch new businesses.

This year, I am on track to have my most successful year ever, all while living a life of freedom, travel, and pretty much anything I desire.

People ask me all the time how I did this and I have to say, it is just the simple system that Anik taught me. That is it. The only thing I added to the mix was my sheer dedication and belief. I had faith. I worked hard and I took action.

I am looking you in the eyes right now and telling you, 'You can do this. This is real. Everything in this book and everything you get with the training at Lurn is absolutely life-changing in ways you cannot even imagine.

The only things you need? Belief. Action. Persistence."

Jimmy is one of our star students because he immediately went to work and worked hard. He always took action and has always been first in line when there is an opportunity to learn. I will never say that his results are typical. I would also never promise you any kind of results at all. That would not be fair.

However, I wanted you to read his story and see all that is possible. He never, ever thought he would be an online entrepreneur.

He did not even know this world exists. He came into it completely fresh. He simply took my system, put it into action, and worked at it until he started making millions.

To this day, as I type this, Jimmy's working the system. He understands that the more he fuels the Circle of Profit, the greater his profits will be!

CHAPTER 29: OUR STUDENT WHO ESCAPED IRAQ, NOW LIVING THE AMERICAN DREAM!

This next story is just marvelous. Zane Baker started with Lurn in 2014 and has become an incredible success in almost no time. What is even more amazing is Zane's story. If you saw him three years ago, you would never predict that he would be an online entrepreneur living the life of his dreams today.

Zane was:

- Born and raised in Baghdad, Iraq
- Spoke English as his second language
- Had zero experience in business
- Had zero experience in online marketing
- A three-year failure at online marketing!

Zane came to us as his last resort. He was ready to give up. He had been through so many other programs to try to learn that he was fed up. He just was not seeing any success.

Zane escaped Iraq a few years ago and settled down in America. He wanted nothing more than to live the American Dream and achieve financial freedom. Of course, to make ends meet, he found a job and started working day and night.

He found himself spending hours in traffic, barely making enough money to pay his bills - and completely drained of his passion.

He wanted more from life. A lot more. He wanted to live a life of complete financial freedom. When he came across the world of online marketing, he was hooked. He immediately began to try. He went through every course he could find. He tried to hire coaches.

But nothing was working!

One day, he came across one of our Lurn training programs. Today he openly says that his entire life changed with that program. He went from not being able to make a dime on the Internet to quitting his day job.

Zane just recently had his first $10,000 month. He was ecstatic, and wanted to write the following letter for you.

In the words of Zane Baker:

"The feeling I had when I made my first $10,000.

Growing up in Iraq, you can imagine the background I come from. I was raised in practically the slums of Iraq. I did not know English. I did not have any business experience or anything. After escaping to America, I did what everyone does: I got a job.

I always knew I wanted more for my life, but I did not know where to turn. I barely knew anyone in the entire country, much less, anyone in business who could help me.

One day, I fell into the world of online marketing. I thought I had my answer, but as it turned out, I didn't. I spent two years and every penny of my savings trying to find a system that actually worked.

Let me tell you, there are hundreds of systems that you can buy online. You have to be very careful.

Then one day, I was scrolling the Internet and I came across Lurn's programs. Something about them just felt right. I really felt that Anik was the mentor I had been searching for. I decided to take a leap of faith and give it a try.

Looking back now, I am so grateful that I had the right mind to do it. Had I missed that opportunity, I would still be stuck in the morning traffic for two hours, even today.

I have followed the Circle of Profit system exactly and have seen nothing but amazing results. I am growing every single month. My email list is now over 20,000 and growing by leaps and bounds every month. I'm also very proud to announce that I just crossed my first $10,000 month in January 2015!

The feeling I had when I made my first $10,000 was of pure relief. I had done it! I was so excited I could not see straight. I officially know now that the day when I am a multi-millionaire and completely free is just a reach away. It is just a matter of continuing to follow the system - and I'm virtually guaranteed to make it!

The system really does work. It works just as Anik says it will. The only thing you need to do is take action. Period. Do not think. Do not question. As Nike says, 'Just do it!'"

Chapter 30: Your Exact Next Steps

First, I want to congratulate you on what you have already done. Take a moment to really be proud of yourself, because most people never make it this far. Everyone loves to talk about all the big things they want to do, but few have the true passion and desire to give it the attention needed.

This book is just step one of the process to turning your passion into $1 million. If you will allow me, I really want to be your head coach and lead you through the entire process. There are two major next steps that will allow you to work together with me and my trainers much more closely.

There are many additional resources of training we can offer you. Some of the resources require a small investment and some of them are free.

Moving forward, I will make a few personal recommendations:

1 – www.Lurn.com - Please explore our website to learn more about the programs we offer and how we can personally help you build your business.

2 – Subscribe to our newsletter. We have an additional free book you can receive by going to www.Lurn.com and simply subscribing to our free newsletter. In this free book, I give you a very guided approach to launching your own information product.

3 – Join our blog community! This is the first step to becoming a part of our Lurn Nation. Please come by our blog, introduce yourself, and absorb the amazing information we have prepared for you.

4 – Enroll in our courses and training. The two programs I recommend the most are:

> **Inbox Blueprint** – Teaches you how to build an email marketing business and provides you with the industry's #1 technology to help you launch your business in less than 60 minutes.
> **www.InboxBlueprint.com**

Publish Academy – Teaches you how to publish your first course online and how to quickly begin producing profits from it. This community is rated the best training and hand-holding coaching you can find when it comes to digital publishing. Please come visit us to learn more at **www.PublishAcademy.com**.

I want to give you a heartfelt thank you for having placed your trust in me and the entire team here at Lurn. It is our mission to help change the lives of at least 1,000 students who dedicate themselves to the digital publishing process.

From here, the only thing you need to do is take action. There will be hard days. You will encounter obstacles. There may even be days that you want to quit.

But don't. These are the very days we invite you to turn to us. We are here to support you in any way we can.

It has been my great honor to bring the digital publishing world into your life. I look forward to many more adventures together!

Anik Singal
CEO, Founder & Lead Fighter
Lurn, Inc.

Remember:

When life pushes you,
stand straight, smile and push it the heck back!

OTHER RESOURCES FROM THE AUTHOR

Books by Anik Singal

Passion to Profit
The 7 Simple Steps to Turning
Your Passion Into Rewarding Profit

Get your free copy here: www.publishacademy.com

The Email Lifeline
How to Increase Your E-Mail Marketing Profits by 300% Using a Simple
Formula

Get a Kindle copy for $0.99 on Amazon

Lurn Online Courses

Inbox Blueprint
For more information please visit www.inboxblueprint.com

Publish Academy
For more information please visit www.publishacademy.com

List Academy
For more information please visit www.listacademy.com

Other Resources

Please visit our Lurn Blog for updates and free content.
www.lurn.com/blog

INDEX